NEWS
REPORTERS
AND
NEWS
SOURCES

NEWS REPORTERS AND NEWS SOURCES

WHAT HAPPENS BEFORE THE STORY IS WRITTEN

HERBERT STRENTZ

IOWA STATE UNIVERSITY PRESS / AMES

HERBERT STRENTZ is dean and associate professor, School of Journalism, Drake University, Des Moines, Iowa. His degrees include the B.A. from Fresno State College, the M.A. from Syracuse University, and the Ph.D. from Northwestern University. His professional experience includes reporting and editing for daily newspapers and a wire service, and he has written several articles for journals in his field.

© 1978 The Iowa State University Press
Ames, Iowa 50010. All rights reserved

Composed and printed by
The Iowa State University Press

First edition, 1978

Library of Congress Cataloging in Publication Data

Strentz, Herbert.
    News reporters and news sources.

    Includes bibliographical references and index.
    1. Reporters and reporting.   I. Title.
PN4781.S78   070.4′3   77–14048
ISBN 0–8138–1885–0

CONTENTS

v

PREFACE

This is a book about what happens *before* news stories are written. A news story does not take form the moment a reporter sits at a typewriter or in front of a microphone. What news will reach the audience has been decided long before the first word is written or spoken. It is not a matter of fate or predestination; it is a matter of the competence of the reporter and the manner in which he or she gathers information.

If this book makes the student journalist, reporter, or news audience more sensitive to the nuances of the reporting process, it will have served its purpose.

Much of the material on the following pages comes from happy associations with colleagues at the *Fresno Bee* in Fresno, California; at the Associated Press in Albany, New York; and during summer employment at the *Minneapolis Tribune*. Much of it reflects also my rewarding work with faculty and students at the Universities of Kentucky and North Dakota, and Drake University.

It may not be obvious, but I hope the book reflects some of the better influences on me by such people as Curtis Mac-Dougall, George Gruner, Steve Aakre, Char Barta Kvernstoen, and Juli Smith Thorson. Dr. MacDougall, professor emeritus at Northwestern University, was chairman of my doctoral committee. Gruner was an assistant city editor at the *Fresno Bee* when I began work there, and he taught me a great deal about news-writing and editing. Now he is the managing editor and one of the "Fresno Four" who served jail terms in a California shield law case. Steve, Char, and Juli represent here the students it has been good to know.

Joe Patrick of the Drake journalism faculty provided many helpful comments in editing the manuscript, and Charles Rose, also of Drake, wrote the section on public relations news sources in Chapter Five.

The book is dedicated to my wife, Joan, and our daughters, Tamara and Laura—partly in apology and partly in thanks for Joan's patience and help in its production.

Because of the topics surveyed in the book, it must be shallow in some areas. I have listed at the end of each chapter some recommended readings and bibliographies intended to provide additional insight to the subjects covered. Many questions are left unanswered. I think that is because of the nature of the questions. Answers to important issues involving the journalist's responsibility in society and the protection of our First Amendment freedoms do not come easily. The absence of easy or final answers, however, is the challenge that makes the profession of journalism worthwhile.

DOONESBURY

by Garry Trudeau

1 | Newsgathering and the power of the press

News reporters may have something in common with the person in a shooting accident who "didn't know the gun was loaded." News stories sometimes take unexpected turns or have consequences that even the reporter finds surprising, shocking, or distressing.

That little analogy is a good way to lead into the main points of this introductory chapter, which are these:

1. The power of the press—roughly translated as the power to shape opinions and to lead to action in a desired direction—should not be understood solely in terms of the editorials, the pronouncements of columnists and commentators, and the news coverage itself.

2. The manner in which a reporter gathers information for a news story may affect his or her news sources and their understanding of the issue under study—just as it certainly affects the content of a news story when that story is written.

3. In deciding whether to cover a newsworthy event, the possible consequences of coverage and publication or broadcast are among the least reliable criteria for decision making. Consequences of the story often are beyond the control of the reporter; the accuracy and relative interest and importance of the

Miss Peach / By Mell Lazarus

Courtesy Mell Lazarus and Field Newspaper Syndicate

news item to readers and viewers are more within the bounds of judgments reporters and editors should be competent to make.

THE POWER OF THE PRESS

A newspaper editorial is written and a mayor is ousted from office; a series of television programs on child abuse results in state legislation requiring physicians to report suspicious cases to the police; the city planning commission denies a request to rezone land after a news story raises questions about the land developer's contributions to a city councilman's campaign. All these are examples of the power of the press, right? Well, maybe.

Then another editorial is written and, despite it, the criticized incumbent is reelected mayor by the largest majority in city history; a television program on inadequacies of the county jail is followed only by the resounding defeat of a bond issue for a new facility; a cogent argument for sound city planning—painstakingly outlined in a series of news articles—is forgotten two weeks after publication. The surprising thing to editors and reporters in these cases may be that the "loaded gun" did *not* go off, that well-documented news coverage of social problems did not generate concern to work for solution of these problems.

In an unprecedented sweep of major awards for news reporting, James Risser of the *Des Moines Register* in 1976 won the Pulitzer Prize, the Raymond Clapper Award, the Worth Bingham Award, and the Sigma Delta Chi Award—all in recognition of his outstanding reporting of corruption in the grain exporting trade. Yet in a talk at Drake University in June 1976, Risser gave what he termed "a somewhat pessimistic assessment" of efforts to reform the grain inspection system:

Grain reform legislation, which has passed both houses of Congress, is now stalled in a Senate-House conference committee. Meaningful reforms are being blocked by powerful vested interests in the grain trade, who oppose the legislation because it would interfere with their ability to continue their criminal conduct. The reforms also are being blocked by a small band of congressmen who are putting petty, parochial concerns above the national interest.

These congressmen are maneuvering to protect private and state-run inspection agencies in their home districts, rather than viewing, on a national scale, the damage this scandal has done to the image of the grain industry and to the image of the U.S. as a grain supplier to the world.

The Agriculture Department, because of its long-standing close association with the big grain firms, is offering no help at all, and has in fact complicated the situation by refusing to recognize that any basic reforms are needed.[1]

Situations like this leave reporters talking to themselves and provide editors a sardonic chuckle when they hear themselves referred to as being among the most powerful men in the community.

Few deny that the news media can shape events through what is reported in the news columns or advocated on the editorial page. But in the wake of such success, reporters and editors may be likened to someone who receives a vaguely worded letter of congratulations and a $50 check in the morning mail. It may give the recipient a good feeling, a sense that something worthwhile has happened. But it may also leave one a trifle confused; it would be nice to understand why one received the accolades, so there might be a chance to do something right again sometime.

One reason for the confusion regarding the concept of the power of the press is that we may take too simplistic a view of the reporting process. Something happens *after* an article is written; therefore, it is argued, it happened *because* the article was written. The problem is compounded because it is still not widely appreciated that the media may serve as societal mirrors far more than they serve as visionaries or prophets. If the media appear to have predictive powers, it may be only because they are faithfully reporting the directions in which society itself is moving.

THE REPORTER AS INTERMEDIARY

If we are to appreciate the role of the news media in our society, we have to recognize that the press can and often does have effect even when editorials, columns, or news stories are neither written nor read. Simply by going about his or her business, by talking with news sources, by gathering information, a reporter exercises "power." The reporter may become an intermediary between news sources, just as the reporter in the more familiar role is an intermediary between news sources and the news audience.

The role of intermediary may be most familiar or most visible in smaller communities where the reporter or editor daily meets with news sources on social, religious, and professional bases. The small-town editor may be a power in his community because he regularly talks with all the community leaders, even if the substance of their conversations is never published. But one sees similar reportorial behavior in larger cities too; reporters may talk with several decision makers in a week's time, pollinating one with ideas from another. Indeed, a reporter may talk with government agencies more than the agencies talk with one another.

Government agencies at the city, county, state, and federal levels at times almost make it a point to act independently of one another, even though they are doing so supposedly in the interest of the same person—the taxpayer. So grand schemes might be drawn up for highway development in Kentucky with little concern for the highway systems in the contiguous states of Illinois, Indiana, Ohio, West Virginia, Virginia, Tennessee, and Missouri. Or, on a smaller scale, city planners in Bakersfield, California, might think of city development without considering what Kern County planners have in mind for zoning just outside the Bakersfield city limits.

The manner in which newspaper beats are assigned is sometimes more logical than the way government agencies operate. Perhaps in Bakersfield, whoever covers city planning also covers county planning. If so, the county and city planners will talk to each other—if only through the reporter—and perhaps contradictions in city and county plans will be discovered, discussed, and remedied without a story's ever being written. The reporter may not even know contradictions exist but may—by simply stopping by the courthouse on a Tuesday afternoon and talking for a while with the county planner—share information necessary for the county to have if there is to be intelligent development where city and county lines meet.

The hypothetical highway scheme in Kentucky provides another illustration of the reporter as intermediary. Reporters for, say, the *Louisville Courier-Journal* should recognize that news stories about highways in Kentucky must consider highways in bordering states, and again the reporter may become an intermediary. His reporting efforts may have effect—greater awareness of regional plans on the part of those doing statewide planning—even before a story is written.

With these illustrations in mind, one question that may have occurred to you already is, How does one distinguish between the role of reporter as intermediary and the role of the reporter as "do-gooder"? For when anyone talks about a reporter exercising influence without ever writing a news story, the next step is a predictable one: The primary role of the reporter might easily be interpreted as the solving of social problems. If a reporter can remedy difficult situations without writing a story, why not do so? The role is a tempting one for at least three reasons:

1. The reporter may decide that the ultimate goal of reporting is social change in a desired direction. If an informed public is to be relied on to provide the change, that is likely to take a lot longer than if the reporter can be a "surrogate public" and lobby for change without necessarily writing news stories day in and day out.

2. For the reporter there is a heady feeling that comes with being at the center of power—whether that center is something as modest as a small-town zoning commission or as awesome as the office of Secretary of State of the United States of America. When anyone becomes a confidante of people wielding such power, it may be easy to understand the troubles they face and consequently cooperate by joining the team and relishing the role of intermediary between centers of power.

3. Most news sources believe, rightly or wrongly, that they understand the "big picture" better than others and may express fears about the "power of the press" to botch up their grand programs. A wrong story here, a misplaced quote there, and, *voila*, the reporter has killed a program that offered great potential for the betterment of society. A reporter who perceives himself as ill informed and unprepared to assume responsibility for

the "great harm" his news stories might do to society may well decide that it is in everyone's best interest to leave the story unwritten.

In simple classroom exercises or discussions it is easy to see how willing young journalists are to adopt the role of Mr. or Ms. Fix-It. Pose a problem in which a reporter is asked to not report a story because (1) someone may be harmed or (2) the problem can be solved just as readily without the notoriety a story might bring. The student's solution, more often than not, will be to not write the story.

CONSEQUENCES OF NEWS STORIES

A problem: James Hennings, 32, a furniture salesman, was arrested ten days ago on a burglary charge. The paper carried a story about his arrest. Now the charges have been dropped, and a second story is warranted. But his wife phones the city desk and argues: "Do you have to print another story? Jim's boss at work was really upset about the story on the burglary arrest, but he's calmed down now and is willing to keep Jim on the job provided there is no more publicity about the thing. If you print the story about the charges being dropped, the whole thing will blow up again and Jim will be fired. We just can't afford to lose this job. Jim's worked so hard. Please don't print the story." What do you tell Mrs. Hennings?

A common classroom answer is to ask for the boss's phone number so the reporter can take Jim off the hook and make things easier for him at work. Another answer is to check out the case—do an investigative job on what led to the arrest and what led to the dismissal of charges. Then if it appears that Jim is indeed innocent, don't do a story; but if something is fishy, write the story.

It occurs to almost no students that Mrs. Hennings may be lying, or that whether she is lying or whether Jim "really" guilty is irrelevant to the decision about running the story. Nor does it occur to many that a phone call from the newspaper may be just the thing to convince the "publicity-shy" boss that Hennings should have been fired right after the arrest.

If the paper has run a story about the arrest, it must run the story about the dismissal of charges. There is a responsibility to the readers and to the record and even to the Hennings family to print the story about dismissal. The possible consequences of not printing the second story include lingering questions in readers' minds about when Hennings will go to trial and possible errors two or three years later when another reporter working on another story about Hennings finds only the clipping about his arrest. Such possibilities are at least as injurious as any imagined consequences from the boss's seeing the story that charges against his employee have been dropped.

The sad fact is that there is no news story that cannot possibly harm or upset some person. To take from a newspaper or a broadcast any story that might have adverse and unintended consequences would be to leave the paper blank and the air time silent.

Glance through a newspaper for "harmless" stories. You are likely to find many that appear harmless: a short obituary about a 75-year-old man who had led a full life; a story announcing an engagement; an item about finalists for homecoming queen; a story simply noting that the city council will meet at 7 P.M. tomorrow. However, the obituary might spark a family feud about the order in which the surviving sons and daughters are listed or whether Roy should have been listed at all, since "We all know how Dad felt about him"; the item about the engagement may come as a surprise to the parents of the boy or girl or to a lover who suddenly finds himself jilted; the homecoming story is certain to hurt the egos of some candidates who may feel "just humiliated"; even the item about the city council meeting might arouse the suspicions of a housewife whose husband has told her he cannot come home for dinner that night because the council's session starts at 4 P.M. and will continue to midnight.

Exaggerated? Perhaps. But consider the assistant city editor who received a phone call from a woman complaining about a Page 1 story about a man, 21, who murdered his brother, 19, with a knife during a family argument. He also cut his mother when she tried to stop the assault in her kitchen. The woman on the phone was the mother, sufficiently recovered from her wound to voice her complaint: The story said she and her mortally wounded son were taken to the county hospital when in fact they were taken to a private hospital. She did not want readers to think they were so poor they had to go to the county hospital!

At least this unexpected complaint can be explained in part

by its source—a grief-stricken mother whose world had been shattered in a kitchen murder (and the hospital named in the story was the wrong one).

The fact that a reporter cannot anticipate all the consequences of his or her story is not an invitation to irresponsible and incomplete news coverage. The point is that the news audience is better served if the decision of whether to publish a story is made in terms of interest, importance, and accuracy.

THE NEWSGATHERING PROCESS

A summary of the discussion of the power of the press, the reporter as intermediary, and the consequences of news stories would include at least this much: It is useful and perhaps necessary for reporters and students of reporting to recognize the subtleties and dynamics of the newsgathering process.

Reporters would be more competent and the news audience better informed if they recognized: (1) How a reporter gathers information determines what ultimately reaches the news audience. (2) Even if some information never reaches the news audience, the reporter may have influenced the direction of public policy—exercised power of the press—by simply asking questions of people in positions of power and serving as an intermediary between news sources.

The challenge to the reporter as intermediary is twofold: (1) The reporter must resist temptations to become part of news events himself or herself at the expense of responsibility to the news audience. (2) The reporter must recognize that the selection of news sources and the questions he or she asks will not only affect the story itself but may also shape the outcome of the issue being reported.

The effects of what the reporter does and what the reporter writes may be unintended, often unperceived, and sometimes unpredictable; nevertheless, they are real and part of the power of the press.

Recommended Readings
    Cater, Douglass. *The Fourth Branch of Government.* New York: Vintage, 1959.
    Cohen, Bernard. *The Press and Foreign Policy.* Princeton: Princeton University Press, 1963.
    Liebling, A. J. *The Press.* New York: Ballantine Books, 1964.
    Reston, James. *The Artillery of the Press.* New York: Harper & Row, 1967.

Rivers, William L. *The Adversaries.* Boston: Beacon Press, 1970.
Sigal, Leon V. *Reporters and Officials: The Organization and Politics of Newsmaking.* Lexington, Mass; D. C. Heath and Company, 1973. See section on references, pp. 201–12.

2 | Pitfalls and pratfalls awaiting the reporter

In the old television detective series *Dragnet,* Jack Webb as Sergeant Joe Friday sought "just the facts." Hundreds of criminals were caught and crimes solved because of Friday's insistence on "just the facts, ma'am"—a line that popped up in enough *Dragnet* shows to become parodied nationwide.

Although that method worked well for Joe Friday, a news reporter is deluding himself or herself and the audience if he or she thinks there always is a collection of information that represents *"just* the facts, ma'am," unaffected by the perceptions of the observer. The reporter and the audience will be better served if the following points are remembered:

1. Different persons see the same event differently.
2. The same person will report the same event selectively and differently depending on his or her audience.
3. The nature of the newsgathering process often determines how "the facts" are reported. Of importance here are: (a) the definition of what is news, (b) the rational nature of news, and (c) the prejudgment of newsworthy events.

What follows in this chapter is an effort to provide you with some appreciation of the news event as the reporter finds it and with some understanding of circumstances that determine what a news reporter reports.

Wordsmith

DIFFERENT PERCEPTIONS BY DIFFERENT OBSERVERS

Because it is easily understood, the fable about the blind men and the elephant is often used to illustrate how people see things differently. You may recall that one blind man felt the elephant's legs and likened the beast to a tree; another felt its tail and called it a rope; a third felt its side and recognized that it was quite like a wall; the one who felt its ear declared it a fan; it was more like a spear to the one who felt its tusk; and the one who felt its trunk knew that, if anything, the pachyderm was most like a snake. Each had a version of the truth; unfortunately, even taken collectively, the versions did not add up to "one elephant."

That's a useful and harmless fable—useful because it makes the point; harmless because it does not arouse the emotional response we might get if we suggested people have differing interpretations of God, the Republican party, Mom, and apple pie.

What makes much reporting difficult is that news sources generally do not intend to deceive or mislead the reporter and the news media audience. Like the men in the fable, they give their honest and—to them—accurate perceptions. That those interpretations may differ from morning to noon or from reporter to reporter is not usually the result of any conspiracy to distort or mislead the reporter and the audience.

People have vested interests, and those interests affect how they see the world. A man does not have to be the incarnation of evil to oppose busing for racial integration of schools. A woman does not have to be simpleminded to oppose the Equal Rights Amendment. A politician does not have to be a Communist dupe to believe in arms control or detente. (Most readers, like the author, might be tempted to add "but it helps" after one or another of those statements—just further evidence of the point we are trying to make here.)

Sometimes it is useful to think of news sources or interest groups as having flags that they figuratively wave. The inscriptions on the banners suggest how the news sources see the world. Members of school boards, for example, have a banner that reads "For the Children." When a reporter asks why the school board took a certain action, the members unfurl the flag and announce, "We did it for the children." Labor unions have a flag that reads "For the Working Man." Former President Nixon's banner read "For National Security" or "For the Presidency." The flags of many city councils read "For the Community." The Boy Scouts do things "For God and Country." (Journalists, of course, do things "For the Public's Right to Know," but that's another story). In reporting on school boards, labor unions, and city councils, a reporter who does not take into account the orientation and interests of the news source is likely to feel misled or lied to when encountering other news sources who have credible but opposing points of view.

Occasionally we may meet people of very high principle who say, "John lied to me, so I'll never trust him again." Or, "If you lie to me just once, I'll never trust you again." Few reporters can afford such high principles. In a month's time they may not have anyone to talk with and will be useless to their employers and their audience. There is a gray area between "lies" and "biased perceptions," either of which may mislead the unwary reporter and the trusting news audience.

If a reporter is to maintain a sense of perspective and some usefulness to employer and audience, he or she must recognize that news sources who might mislead the reporter do not always do so deliberately. The point is driven home hundreds of times a day: by copy editors who insist that an address given by police be checked against the phone book, city directory, or other sources; by reporters who still check the dictionary for the spelling of a word, even though a newsroom colleague has spelled it for them; by reporters who recognize that the defense attorney's interpretation of a judge's ruling may not be the same as the prosecuting attorney's. It is easy to demonstrate that different people will see the same event differently. Walter Lippmann in his classic essay on stereotypes noted: "For the most part we do not see and then define, we define first and then we see."[1] To paraphrase Lippmann, we often see what we want to see or hear what we want to hear.

DIFFERENT VERSIONS TO DIFFERENT AUDIENCES

While it may be easy to recognize such behavior at least in others, we may be less sensitive to the notion that the same person may report the same event selectively and differently, depending on the audience. This complicates the work of the reporter, who must contend not only with differing reports from different persons but also with differing reports from the same person. Here are two simple illustrations of such behavior:

1. A high school girl, invited to the senior prom, might report that event selectively to different persons. With her schoolmates her discussion of her prospective date may depend on her or her date's relative popularity, whether the person to whom she is talking will also be going to the dance, whether she would have preferred to go with someone else and whether that is known. With her parents she may stress different values by talking of the date's manners, upbringing, and status to one parent and his driving ability to another. Combining the different descriptions of the date may give us a mixture of Robert Redford, Billy Graham, and A. J. Foyt, and the view of the date may be as accurate as the fable's composite elephant.

2. A school board member might explain support for a $1 million bond issue in different ways to different audiences. To the voters it might be presented as a difficult decision but a necessary step—unfurl that flag—"For the Children." To teachers it might be presented as a move toward improved teaching conditions in lieu of higher salaries. To other board members it might be interpreted as an opportunistic move because chances for passage of the bond issue appear to be better now than they will be in a few years. To a spouse the bond issue might be represented as a chance to accomplish something worthwhile, to have something to show after all these years of school board meetings.

It must be noted that in both cases the different accounts to different audiences are not necessarily contradictory. But the pictures the different listeners receive are indeed varied, and the sum of all the pictures still may not equal the whole.

If accounts of high school dates and bond issues can vary so easily, should we be surprised when political candidates are reported as saying different things to different audiences? Such supposed doubletalk is "surprising" for at least two reasons: (1) We do not take into account the audience and its effect on the speaker. (2) Having already reported or read about a candidate's stand on an issue, we now must modify our understanding to take into account the candidate's latest comments. The world becomes more complex, and that is unsettling—partly because of the difficulty in distinguishing between outright lies by a candidate and changes in perspective forced on him by his audience.

(The idea that the audience influences what is said by a speaker is a relatively recent discovery; at least that facet of the communication process did not receive much attention until recently. In 1963 Raymond Bauer wrote of how the composition of the audience might dictate what a speaker said.[2] That was a radical twist from the popular approach, which long emphasized the power of the speaker or the mass media over the audience.)

INFLUENCE OF REPORTER ON SOURCE

Logically, if the audience may influence what the speaker says, the reporter may influence what the news source says in much the same fashion. The news source may respond to the reporter's questions not only in terms of the source's self-interest but also in terms of his perception of the reporter. A woman reporter interviewing citizens about the Equal Rights Amendment is likely to get responses different from those to a male reporter. A black reporter interviewing a city council member about racial segregation in urban housing is likely to receive information different from what a white reporter would receive. A reporter who appears sympathetic to a news source's predicament is likely to be given responses different from those to a reporter who is perceived as neutral or hostile. It is easy to add to this list. The point is that who the reporter is and how he or she is perceived by the news source may often determine what information ultimately reaches the audience—*particularly if the reporter is unaware of his influence on the news source.*

Several years ago James Wrightson, now an associate editor with the McClatchy Newspapers in Sacramento, talked about how he and Charles Hurley covered the Fresno County courthouse. His description of their reporting styles and their influence on news sources went something like this: "Hurley and I work differently. When Chuck goes into an office, people pull out their pictures of their families and show them to Chuck. They have a nice time. They're happy to see him. When I come in they say, 'Here comes the wrecker.' But we both get our stories."

There was no question of either reporter's competence. Each had a reporting style he was aware of and comfortable with. Each recognized a need for occasional changes in that style— for Hurley to deal with people on a less personal level at times and for Wrightson to vary his techniques, too.

Reporters' styles may change not only from day to day but within interviews, within newsgathering situations. A good example of a reporter's careful probing to get information from a news source is Jack Perkin's interview of Sirhan Sirhan, the killer of U.S. Senator Robert F. Kennedy.[3] Early in the interview Perkins was probing, providing the audience with information and establishing rapport with the news source. Midway through the interview he became more questioning and critical. Toward the end he began to ask questions and make observations that would have been counterproductive earlier.

Some of Perkins's questions early in the interview:

> PERKINS: Sirhan, for two years before the assassination, you were reading a great deal about the occult, mind over matter. You were doing experiments . . . can you tell us about some of those?
> SIRHAN: Well, as I said in court about the . . . candle experiment, where you would concentrate on seeing the flame on the candle as being any color you want it to become. You just look at the flame and think red, for instance, long enough and you will see a red flame, and then a green flame, and then yellow or any . . . and then you get to the point where you see any color you want. . . .
> PERKINS: You consider yourself a poor person?
> SIRHAN: Yes, sir, I do. And I wish that I wouldn't be here on this program. . . .
> PERKINS: When you came to this country you had bought the American Dream, hadn't you?
> SIRHAN: I bought it 100 per cent . . . 100 per cent.
> PERKINS: Were you disillusioned later with it?
> SIRHAN: Only after the Arab-Israeli War, sire, when I started. I had no job. I tried . . . I sincerely tried to find a job. After I was dismissed from school and after this Arab-Israeli War and the continuing fighting in the Middle East now, I had no identity. No . . . no hope, no goal, nothing to strive for and I suddenly gave up. There was no more American Dream for me. I couldn't buy it any more.

Then as Perkins began to get into the details of the assassination, he asked tougher questions and at times seemed incredulous at Sirhan's answers. Perkins at one point almost apologized for asking a difficult question and then became still tougher in the questioning:

> PERKINS: Sirhan, the obvious question is, of course, did you go to the Ambassador Hotel that Sunday to case the place, to plan, to plot, to wait, stake it out, find out where you could shoot him?
> SIRHAN: Sir, I know this sounds unbelievable but I went there just to see senator Kennedy.
> PERKINS: All right, Sirhan, now on the night of the assassination you said you went to the Ambassador Hotel, had a few drinks and then you said you were too drunk to drive home, didn't you?
> SIRHAN: Yes sir, I did.

Sirhan and Perkins then discussed the assassination and Sirhan's contention that he didn't recall a thing until he was at the police station. Perkins noted that Sirhan didn't ask why the police were holding him:

> PERKINS: You were being held in the middle of the night at a police station with officers all around you and you were handcuffed and it must have occurred to you to ask "Why am I here?"
> SIRHAN: I wish I could have. I wish I could have.
> PERKINS: But you didn't? . . . Which, of course, makes it look as if you knew why you were there.

Perkins later mentioned Sirhan's notebook in which, before the assassination, Sirhan wrote that RFK must die or must be sacrificed:

> SIRHAN: I know, sir, that they are my writings. It's my handwriting, my thoughts, but I don't remember them.
> PERKINS: Well, did you only write them when you were in great fits of anger?
> SIRHAN: I must have been, sire, I must have been. They are the writings of a maniac.
> PERKINS: They're the writings of Sirhan Sirhan.

Perkin's interview of Sirhan Sirhan ended with the assassin in tears, after expressing wishes that Senator Kennedy were still alive and that there would be peace in the Middle East. Perkins again was in a sympathetic role, having asked questions about Sirhan's family.

In total the interview provides a picture of an assassin who changed world history—a slight, befuddled man awaiting transfer to San Quentin Prison. Perkins generally was unobtrusive during the interview, asking questions in an order and demeanor that would provide the audience with more insight into this man and the event. A less-skilled reporter—one not as sensitive to how the news source was responding and not as well prepared for the interview—would not have provided the insights to Sirhan Sirhan that Perkins did.

In addition to the individual reporter's influence on news sources and newsgathering (which will be further discussed in the next chapter), there are institutional factors that determine what news is gathered and how that news is reported. As noted earlier, those factors include definitions of news, the rational nature of news, and the prejudgment of newsworthy events.

DEFINITIONS OF NEWS

News reporting textbooks list the criteria used to determine if an event is news. A beginning reporting student can list these criteria quickly: human interest, timeliness, conflict, proximity, consequence, and prominence. Experienced reporters may not use these terms but may offer working definitions such as, "News is what I say it is," "News is what is reported in the papers," "News is something you know today that you didn't know yesterday."

Whether you take the codified versions of news from the textbooks or a working reporter's seat-of-the-pants definition, it is axiomatic that how news is defined determines what is reported: i.e., if an editor decides that someone is prominent, that individual's activities will receive more attention than those of someone considered less prominent.

The point is not lost on those seeking to use the media. They recognize that to merit news coverage—to use the media to gain attention for themselves or their ideas—they must contrive events or otherwise convince editors that their subject matter is newsworthy. And they often do this by exploiting those criteria listed in the journalism textbook: human interest (have the movie starlet pose with an exotic pet); timeliness (schedule a press conference at a time convenient to a newspaper's deadline); conflict (threaten to pollute a city's drinking water with LSD or suggest other bizarre activities as protestors did in the days before the 1968 Democratic National Convention in Chicago); proximity (establish a good local tie between the cause and the community); prominence (promote the status of the client by suggesting widespread public interest in him or her or contrive appearances with people already defined as prominent by the news media); consequence (suggest that many people will be affected).

It follows that if someone wants to keep an item out of the news media, he or she simply reverses the procedures and convinces the news reporter that the individual or event is not newsworthy: human interest ("There's nothing new about this; people are divorced every day"); timeliness ("Oh, that happened a month ago. You mean you just found out about it?"); proximity ("I don't think there's any local interest in this"); prominence ("Most of the people in the city don't know who I am and could not care less about what happens to me"); consequence ("This is strictly between my wife and me, no one else should be concerned").

While definitions of the news may not be found inscribed on the walls of the nation's newsrooms, the people who want to use the media are well aware of the working definitions of news and have often manipulated the media to their advantage.

Any discussion of the definition of news must recognize the relative nature of "news." Such concepts as human interest and prominence certainly are relative terms. Stories that might be lost in the back pages of a Thursday or Friday paper may receive front-page play on a Monday because that day often is considered a "slow day"—partly since government agencies, the source of much news, are just beginning the week. Theodore Roosevelt discovered this more than 70 years ago when he became one of the first presidents to use the news media to his advantage.

If news releases can be controlled by news sources to gain more attention, they can also be timed to gain minimal notice. For example, controversial government reports that have to be released sooner or later may be released during the summer holidays when public attention to the media is lower or when attention is riveted elsewhere—perhaps even on an event contrived by the sources to attract attention. Generally, however, the relative nature of what is news is the outcome of a process of judgments by reporters and editors in considering the day's events and not the result of schemes by news sources. For example, a nursing home fire in which more than 60 people die certainly is an event of national or worldwide interest. Yet such a fire at the Golden Age Rest Home near Fitchville, Ohio, made few front pages in the country on the November 1963 day when John F. Kennedy was assassinated.

Many of the definitions of news, like its relative nature, have been fundamentally unchanged since James Gordon Bennett popularized the content of newspapers in the 1830s. Bennett's *New York Herald* was the best example of why the Penny Press of that era was called "A Press for the Masses."[4]

It may be too sweeping to suggest that changes in the definition of what is news reflect changes in society. Yet a case can be made along those lines for the relatively recent refinements in the prominence and conflict categories of news. The concept of prominence was reshaped during the political turmoil of the early 1950s; the concept of conflict was reanalyzed after the civil disturbances and riots of the 1960s.

Under the traditional definition of news, what a United States senator said was news. It was news because of his prominence, because it often was timely, and because the statements of such a public official could be expected to have effects on others. Senator Joseph McCarthy recognized that his position gave him virtually unquestioned access to the news media. He used that access to warn of what he called Communist infiltration of the federal government; to question the loyalty of General George C. Marshall (now widely acknowledged as one of the great Americans of the past 200 years) and lesser public employes; and generally to nurture the fear, distrust, suspicion, and ill will that are embraced by what we now call "the McCarthy era."[5]

The number of Communists McCarthy said he had uncovered in the State Department and elsewhere varied from speech to speech, but discrepancies went unquestioned. The news media had trouble enough keeping up with McCarthy's new pronouncements and accusations; the existing definitions of news allowed for little questioning or interpretation of McCarthy's charges by reporters. His prominence as a senator also gave him a considerable edge in gaining media attention in his intimidation of lower-ranking federal employes.

By the time the McCarthy tumult had run its course, the news media had at least begun to redefine the concept of prominence as a criterion for news coverage. That facet of the definition of news was broadened to make acceptable the practice of including in news stories questions about the veracity of a prominent source. Questions could be raised by other sources or by reporters who matched a source's comments against the record or against previous statements. It was recognized that mere transmission of a prominent person's statements might be irresponsible reporting.

While the McCarthy era often is cited as the primary reason for this change in the definition of news, the idea certainly was not new. Curtis MacDougall's reporting textbook *Interpretative Reporting*,[6] first published in the 1930s, upset some by its notion of interpreting the news. The report of the Commission on Freedom of the Press in 1947 noted the responsibility of the news media to report not only the fact truthfully but also the truth behind the fact.[7] By that the commission meant that news events should be reported not as isolated incidents but in a context that enables the reader to better understand what is happening in society.

The conflict approach to news does not always place a violent event or argument in a useful context. The concept of conflict as a criterion for news came under analysis in the 1960s when editors and others sifted through the ashes of urban centers after fires and riots and wondered what went wrong. Editors seemed to agree on at least two points: (1) they had covered their black communities inadequately and were surprised by the extent of the violence unleashed in their cities; (2) while they might condemn the violence, they recognized the legitimate social and economic grievances of blacks in the United States.

What might the news media do? One suggestion was to lessen the emphasis on conflict as a criterion for newsworthiness. If the riots and civil disturbances merited news coverage, it was reasoned, so did some of the causes of the unrest, such as discrimination against a sizable portion of the urban population. News coverage of the causes of unrest, it was thought, might prevent future riots by helping to solve problems before they reached the explosive stage. Also the conflict approach to news coverage gave prime news space and time to those urging violence and often might ignore those working for nonviolent solutions to the nation's problems. The conflict criterion of news coverage might give the advantage to the crackpot with a threat to blow up the city hall and ignore the person or organization with a low-key plan for reducing unemployment.

Changing the definitions of news, of course, was not a panacea. Decades later, public officials continue to mislead the public. When their pronouncements are matched against the record, they say the record is in error. And while the media may not wait for conflict to arise before social problems are considered, ample social problems remain for all the media to cover. In both cases, however, the redefinitions of news have changed what is reported. How news is defined determines what is reported, and because of the changes in the definition of news, today's news audience should have more useful information available to it.

THE RATIONAL NATURE OF NEWS

Those of us on the outside looking in at government assume that policy is the product of rational decision-making by a handful of men, just as those outside newspapers looking in assume that news is the product of rational decision-making by a handful of men.
—Ben Bagdikian[8]

Of the traditional ingredients of a news story—Who, What, When, Where, Why, How—one of the most troubling for the reporter and perhaps most misleading for the reader is Why. The problem is that in answering the Why the journalist tries to explain human behavior and offer the reader easy answers to questions that continue to befuddle psychiatrists, psychologists, and others in the behavioral sciences.

The reporter seeks completeness in news stories. Why did President Carter make that comment? Why did the court rule as it did? Why did the man hold up the store? These are important questions, and the answers may determine the direction of government policy and the course society takes in solving important problems.

The difficulty for the reporter, however, is that the answer to Why is not always available. The person involved in the news story may not know why he acted as he did; yet the reporter offers explanations. Explanations are demanded by copy editors, who see holes in stories that lack the answer to Why, and by the news audience itself, which may be comforted by the availability of rational explanations for irrational acts. Such explanations may make the world a bit more understandable and less frightening. It is unsettling to think that forces beyond our control may lash out at our safety or at our families without warning and without explanation. For the potentially troubled reader, the reporter seeks to provide explanations.

Consider this hypothetical news story, not unlike some seen now and then in the press:

> A 16-year-old boy was held by police today on charges that he murdered his parents last night by shooting them with a shotgun he had received as a Christmas present. Police said the youth killed his parents (Why) because he was not allowed to use the family car after receiving a ticket for speeding.

So there is the explanation, and most of us read stories and do not ask another question. If you reflect on it for a moment and still believe the explanation for the double murder is satisfactory, it is likely you will be a rather permissive parent.

Explanations are needed in news stories, but the desire for rationality—the assurance of some predictability in human affairs—does shape what is reported.

James McCartney of the Knight Newspapers' Washington, D.C., Bureau, was city editor of the *Chicago Daily News* when he talked about how irrational events are filtered by rational reporters and served to readers, perhaps overstating the case.

> We don't know a lot about most of what we put in the paper . . . we don't know anything . . . we don't know about what happened on the west side. Most of what is in the paper comes from irrational people but becomes rational because it filters through rational reporters and copy editors and maybe a rational editor, if you've got one.[9]

To caution readers about the explanations in news stories, reporters attribute information to news sources. The boy did not kill his parents because they would not give him the car: *police said* that might be the explanation. The point remains, however, that the desire for explanations that make the world more understandable and less threatening often shapes what is reported by newsmen.

PREJUDGMENT OF NEWSWORTHY EVENTS

The reporter's work is sometimes made easier (although not necessarily more accurate and more informative) by knowing just what story he or she will find or what story the editors expect. Reporting becomes a game of hide and seek; the reporter knows what he or she is looking for and is not satisfied until it is found.

When an assignment is most specific, the hide-and-seek approach is helpful. "Get Jones's reaction to the district attorney's charge." "What does the union negotiator say to management's latest offer?" Such assignments often are handed to reporters with the understanding that they will have failed if they do not produce the desired information. The reporter knows what he or she is looking for, and the assignment is made easier because of that.

On the other hand, the reporter's responsibility to the audience for informed and accurate reporting can be damaged when the reporter prejudges the story and "knows" what will be discovered before the search for information even begins. There are many reasons for such prejudgment of news, including the incompetence of the reporter, but our discussion will be limited to three related problems that sometimes shape the content of the news: labeling, herd instinct or pack journalism, and tunnel vision.

Labeling

Representative Richard Brademas of Indiana is known as "Mr. Education." Physicist Dr. Edward Teller is "the father of the H-bomb." Richard Nixon was at various times "tricky Dick," "the old Nixon," and "the new Nixon." John F. Kennedy's White House was "Camelot." Relations between the United States and the Soviet Union are conveniently collected under one label, "detente." Women's rights activists at one time were "bra burners" and later "libbers."

Affixing such labels to individuals, issues, or movements condenses them to manageable size. The labeling process does double duty for the reporter by summarizing in a word or phrase why an individual or issue became newsworthy and indicating what the shape of future coverage should be.

Labeling, while saving time and space, may turn a complex individual human being into a unidimensional cardboard character or convert a complicated social issue into a slogan suitable for shouting. Reporters who cover such individuals and issues may prejudge what they will find on the basis of what has already been reported and emphasized. Consequently news stories only reinforce stereotypes and offer the readers or viewers no new insights or observations. Society, its supposed leaders, and its issues are presented as caricatures under the guise of news coverage. Easy explanations and facile answers are offered, sometimes at the expense of informed news audiences and intelligent discussion.

During the Republican primary campaigns in the spring of 1976, President Gerald Ford finally beat down one controversial issue raised by his opponent Ronald Reagan by simply boycotting the use of one label—"detente"—which had become a catchword for all nonhostile relations with the Soviet Union. Ford had trouble explaining to Reagan's satisfaction how he could be opposed to Soviet domination of the free world and still favor detente. He finally gave up trying to explain and announced that the word "detente" simply would not be used any more by him or his administration. There were two noteworthy things here: (1) the President of the United States thought he could avoid controversial issues by avoiding the use of one word; (2) he was right. When Ford stopped using the word, he no longer had to explain it, and neither the press nor Reagan could provide a satisfactory substitute label.

Consider another instance of labeling. The women's rights movement early was labeled as an assembly of "bra burners," and a curious thing happened in the reporting of their rallies. If in some rare early instance a brassiere were burned, that was reported. If no brassiere were burned, that would be reported too—"No bras were burned, however." The news coverage, so practiced in labeling, reinforced the label by reporting its absence, as though that were a surprise and not evidence that the label was inappropriate.

The labels "pro" and "con" may also be deceiving at times, when reporters try to simplify coverage of issues by dividing news sources into those two camps and reporting "both sides" of an issue. Sometimes there are more than two sides to an issue; or the issue may consist of a choice from among several options, none of which is entirely satisfactory.

As indicated, labels persist because they simplify and organize our environment. It is next to impossible for the news reporter to avoid using labels, but the news audience is better served when the reporter recognizes problems inherent in the labeling process and does not let labels affixed by others dictate coverage of the event.

Herd Instinct, Pack Journalism

One lesson taught many times in life is that, generally speaking, it is safer to follow the crowd and not take off on one's own. At its best, such behavior provides a learning experience for neophytes blessed with wise elders and promises the safety inherent in unified action or reaction. At its worst, the tendency toward conformity may mean that no questions are asked and no new experiences are provided. If the crowd is going the wrong way, it will continue to do so; there is no self-correcting mechanism.

In news reporting, herd instinct—sometimes called pack journalism—means news coverage defined almost exclusively in terms of what news is being covered. If that sounds circular, it is. Topics are defined as being newsworthy because they are being covered by other news media.

Some content of the news around the nation may be dictated by what is covered by one or two reporters for one or two respected newspapers or networks and then picked up by the wire services. Reporters for other media then scramble as best they can to get their version—their own exclusive—of what is being covered or reported by leaders of the pack.

The working day for many reporters begins with reading and viewing that others are covering. Pity the reporter on the campaign trail who does not include in his story—if not in his lead—what the Associated Press or others cover and emphasize. The boss reads or views other media too. Not only is there pressure to report what others are reporting, but a reporter who starts on his own—following what he presumes to be a good story—might be stopped in his tracks by an editor who asks, "If this is such a good story, why are we the only ones doing it?"

Such doubts crossed the minds of *Washington Post* editors when they seemed alone in coverage of Watergate; Seymour Hersh faced that question when he sought publication of his stories on the My Lai massacre; James Risser, in his coverage of the grain export scandal, at times found himself talking with federal employees who might have thought reporters were an endangered species because they had seen so few of them.

Examples of pack journalism are found in Timothy Crouse's book about the coverage of the 1972 election, *The Boys on the Bus.*

Peer pressure and expectations of editors may shape what a reporter writes. Often there are good reasons for consensus as to what the story or the lead is. On the other hand, many of the major news stories of recent years are significant because they were developed by reporters who not only were working on their own but may have been thought by some colleagues to be headed in an entirely wrong direction.

Tunnel Vision

Webster's *Third New International Dictionary* defines tunnel vision as "a field of vision of 70 percent or less from the straightahead position resulting in elimination of the peripheral field." Applying that physiological approach to journalism, we take tunnel vision to include such sins as reporting with little breadth or perspective and narrowing one's perception of what is newsworthy to that which one was looking for in the first place.

Reporters who cover only the intent of legislation and not its potential impact suffer from tunnel vision. So do sports writers who note only the strengths of the home team, and editors who truly believe that the new shopping center will be the greatest thing ever for our city.

Reporters may develop tunnel vision over a period of years of contact with the same news source. If so, the reporter may see the newsworthy event only from the point of view of the news source, giving little credence to the views of others.

The process of stereotyping leads to tunnel vision. Consider what happened at a late 1960s rally against the Vietnam War. A journalism professor and some friends thought it odd they did not see a single bearded person at the rally. They scanned the crowd but could not find the stereotyped protester. A reporter and photographer for the local paper had better luck. They somehow managed to find a bearded person in the crowd, and his was the photograph that made the front page of the day's paper.

A key to manipulating the media is simply to know what reporters are looking for. If news sources give it to them, they may be able to shape the coverage they want.

Former Vice President Spiro T. Agnew knew he was guaranteed wide coverage any time he used an alliterative phrase to characterize the news media or foes of the Nixon administration. So when Agnew or his aides wanted attention, they contrived a phrase like "nattering nabobs of negativism," knowing reporters would seize on that. Political writer Jules Witcover quotes an Agnew speech writer:

This was all fairly conscious. It's amusing, titil-
lating, interesting, exciting, to give writers color and
bite in speeches. That's how you get attention. And
above all in a good-natured fashion. That was the
idea . . . what he was doing was calling attention to
his message, and the alliteration and the big words
captured exactly what we intended. Then the press
went overboard on them. After they did that, you
just leave it and do something else.[10]

A natter, by the way, is a chat, trivial conversation, or gripe.
A nabob is defined variously as a mogul, a very rich man, or a
European who became rich in India. Negativism is the sort of
attitude reporters should have toward tunnel vision.

Labeling, herd instinct, and tunnel vision are not forms of
behavior peculiar to journalists. But such traits are particularly counterproductive when displayed by reporters with the
responsibility of telling others what is happening in society.

Recommended Readings
   Balk, Alfred, and Boylan, James, eds. *Our Troubled Press.* Bos-
ton: Little, Brown and Company, 1971.
   Columbia Journalism Review, Columbia University, New York
10027; cumulative index, vols. I–IX, covers Fall 1961 through Winter
1970–71.
   Crouse, Timothy. *The Boys on the Bus.* New York: Ballantine
Books, 1973.
   MacDougall, A. Kent, ed. *The Press: A Critical Look from the
Inside.* Princeton, N.J.: Dow Jones Books, 1972.
   (More), 750 Third Avenue, New York, 10017
   Nieman Reports, Harvard University, Cambridge, Mass. 02138
   Strentz, Herbert; Starck, Kenneth; Anderson, David L.; and Ghig-
lione, Loren. *The Critical Factor: Criticism of the News Media in
Journalism Education.* Journalism Monograph No. 32, Association for
Education in Journalism, 1974. See selected bibliography, pp. 34–40.

3 | Interviewing

This chapter rests on two assumptions: (1) If a reporter prepares for an interview and asks good questions, he or she will probably get a better story than if he or she does not prepare and asks poor questions. (2) How a reporter gathers information determines what information from the news source ultimately reaches the news media audience.

The questions arise: If these assumptions are sound—and they seem obvious to the point of being simplistic—why do reporters not prepare, why do they ask poor questions, and why does the newsgathering process often get in the way of good reporting? Much of what follows tries to answer these questions.

Interviewing in this discussion is almost synonymous with asking questions. Viewed in this way, interviewing is pervasive in journalism. We can avoid many difficulties if we recognize that some popular forms of the interview—the late night talk show on television, the relaxed visit to a dignitary's hideaway for an exclusive story, the man-on-the-street reaction to a news event—differ markedly from most of the interviewing involving news reporters and their sources.

Perhaps because it follows the popular concept of "the interview," a college-level workbook asks, "What devices can a reporter use to put at ease a person he or she is interviewing?" That question is misleading for at least two reasons:

1. It assumes that a person being interviewed should or can be put at ease, and this often is not the case. Many newsgathering situations are tense, uncomfortable, hurried, perhaps

joyous, or, more often, sad; "being at ease" might be totally inconsistent with what is happening. Newsgathering often occurs
during times of stress—a political candidate has to defend his
welfare plan, a policeman explains why he did or did not fire
his revolver at a fleeing burglary suspect, an elderly man who
has never been interviewed by a reporter is asked to explain
what inflation means to him. Tension comes with the territory.
In the TV talk show or many of the other forms of arranged interviews, however, the goals often are to be entertaining and to
put the news source in a good light. In many newsgathering
situations the emphasis should be on getting information important to the reader or viewer, and—to belabor the point—it
often is impossible to be at ease in such situations.

2. The question implies that there are certain gimmicks
or "devices" a reporter can use to put any subject at ease before
extracting the story: (a) smile politely, (b) introduce yourself,
(c) "Mind if I smoke?" (d) exhibit interest in person and/or
subject, (e) offer news source a comfortable chair, (f) take notes
unobtrusively, (g) ask question—"Was that your kid out playing
in the traffic?" (or something equally unnerving).

There are no gimmicks or devices in interviewing, any more
than there is a set formula for how to write a news story. Interviewing is difficult work. The reporter is under pressure to at
least (1) understand what the news source is saying, (2) place
what the news source is saying in perspective with what the
source has said before or with what the reporter knows to have
happened before, (3) think about what question logically follows what the news source is now saying, (4) evaluate the newsworthiness of material the source is providing, (5) seek to de-

termine consistency in the information the source is providing by asking the same question in a different way, and (6) do all of this in a manner that will maximize the amount of newsworthy material to be made available to the reader, viewer, or listener.

Here is an example of some good questioning, taken from a *CBS Reports* program, "The Case of the Plastic Peril." In this segment Correspondent Morton Dean is interviewing a chemist about research on the effects of vinyl chloride on employees in the plastics industry.

> DR. IRVING TABERSHAW: Well, I . . . we've demonstrated that there is a . . . as favorable a mortality ratio working in the industry as you would expect in any population at work. Secondly, we found that there was an increase in . . . in cancer. And I can't characterize how much of an increase, because numbers are so small that we cannot really describe them as significant or not. But there is a trend for the workers in this study to have a little more cancer than we would have expected.
> DEAN: Dr. Tabershaw, would you work in a plant working with vinyl chloride today?
> DR. TABERSHAW: You said "today," Mr. Dean. I think, in the plants that are cleaned up, the plants that are . . . are properly controlled, I would give serious consideration to working in them.
> DEAN: Are there any such plants?
> DR. TABERSHAW: I really don't know. But I assume and I presume that plant conditions can be and, I think, are being controlled to the extent of making it safe to work in them.
> DEAN: Well, what is that safe level?
> DR. TABERSHAW: I wish I knew, Mr. Dean.[1]

This brief exchange is worth reviewing because it is a rare example of good interviewing. It is interesting not because of any imagined battle between the forces of right (CBS) and the minions of evil (in this case the vinyl chloride industry). It is interesting because Morton Dean was hard at work, asking questions that had to be asked if the viewer was to be adequately informed. The need for the questions about the existence of any "properly controlled" plants and the safe chemical level for employees is obvious once the questions are asked. Unfortunately, too many reporters and too many viewers would have been satisfied to have ended the questions right after Dr. Tabershaw said he would give serious consideration to working in safe vinyl chloride plants.

For an example of needless or poor questions, consider a news report in the aftermath of a tornado that struck a small Canadian town in the Province of Quebec in July 1975, killing two small children. The children had received the last rites of the Catholic Church from the same priest who had baptized them a year or so before. The TV reporter asked the grieving (zoom in for close-up) priest, "How did it feel?"

It is one of the puzzles of modern journalism that reporters continue to ask such questions—questions that produce no useful information for viewers and, worse yet, may delude them into thinking they have some information when they know nothing that was not apparent before the question was asked. As one might expect, the priest was unable to answer the question, eliminating any lingering doubt viewers might have had that the death of loved ones is not pleasant to contemplate.

Concern with questions should be paramount in the reporter's mind. The quality of the questions asked will determine how good the news story is. Unfortunately, there are so many barriers against asking good questions that people who ask them run the risk of becoming social pariahs. The many pressures against asking good questions pose additional obstacles to the reporter working to get worthwhile information from a news source.

Consider the many little maxims that helped socialize you: "Little children should be seen and not heard"; "Ask a silly question and you get a silly answer"; "You can be thought a fool by saying nothing or open your mouth and prove it"; and "Silence is golden" but "Curiosity killed the cat." These and others are anecdotal evidence of social constraints against speaking up—against asking questions. By the time a child reaches the fifth grade, she has probably learned that if she asks a question (1) her classmates are likely to think she is merely trying to get the teacher's attention, or (2) she runs the risk of alienating the teacher by displaying her ignorance. Silence is not only golden; it is safe.

Consider what we might call "the sociology of the question." What are the risks, what are the rewards in our society for asking questions? The risks are many. Asking a question may be a sign of ignorance, that you may not have grasped the point, that you missed what is obvious to everyone else (or at least others have the good sense not to ask the question). Asking a question singles you out. You have changed the communication patterns and altered whatever relationships existed between you and others involved in the exchange of information.

In 1963 Robert Gray, a good reporter for the Associated Press, returned from an Albany press conference with New York Governor Nelson Rockefeller with an anecdote about question-asking. Rockefeller had just returned from his Argentine villa where he had honeymooned with his second wife, Happy Murphy. The coterie of Capitol reporters in Albany wanted to know about the vacation: How was Argentina? Did the governor and Mrs. Rockefeller II have a nice time? How was the weather? Then Gray asked his question: "Governor, how will marrying the divorced mother of four affect your chances for your party's presidential nomination?"

As Gray told it, the other reporters drew away from him. Isolated, he received a short, curt, and maybe surly answer from the governor, who until then was having a nice time with his friends from the press. So it is not only in the classroom that there may be pressures against asking questions that should be asked.

(For the record, it might be noted that Rockefeller did not receive the GOP nomination in 1964. The newlyweds' first child was born at the time of the California primary, which Rockefeller narrowly lost to Arizona Senator Barry Goldwater—the eventual GOP nominee.)

Asking a question may be upsetting or threatening to the news source in other ways. Asking a question may suggest to the news source that he has not made his point clear. You do not need much experience in education before you encounter the teacher who is exasperated because, after three lectures and two assigned readings, a student still asks questions about a presumably closed issue. The question may be threatening because it indicates that—whatever the reason—the teacher did not make his or her point clear. And making the point clear is what many teachers are paid to do. Unfortunately, students may soon learn not to ask questions even if they do not understand. The end result often is a teacher who next becomes exasperated because after the presentation of all the material no one has any questions to ask!

Questions may be threatening also because they may suggest to the news source that his view on an issue is not the only one, that alternative—even contrary—points of view may be valid. Having made his point clear, a news source may be alarmed that reporters or others still entertain differing opinions.

Consider an episode from the 1960 presidential election when John F. Kennedy's Roman Catholicism was an issue to many people. Dr. Glenn Archer of Protestants and Other Americans United for Separation of Church and State (POAU) gave an anti-Kennedy, anti-Roman Catholic speech in Fresno, California. It was in a fundamentalist church, and just as Dr. Archer sat down—unburdened of his warnings against popery in the White House—a young man stood and asked, "Is Dr. Archer going to submit to questions or is he going to get away with thinking we all agree with him?"

Archer shouted: "Everywhere I go there are people like you, trying to disrupt my work!" There were no questions, and the presiding minister asked everyone to "return to the Spirit of Christ," forgetting the many questions He had asked.

While casting stones at news sources and peer groups for their roles in discouraging good questions, we might consider, too, the obstacles the reporter creates. Too often, necesssary questions are not asked because the reporter thinks he or she knows the answer. The *Baltimore Sun* published what it considered an expose on Governor Marvin Mandel's misuse of state helicopters. The investigative reporter found evidence that the governor had used the state planes for private and political reasons. William Schmick, the *Sun* city editor, decided it was not necessary to ask the governor about the expose because it was all a matter of public record. Having the goods on the governor, the *Sun* went to press. Well, the case was not that airtight, and the governor had some reasonable answers the reader should have had at the same time the *Sun* presented the "evidence." A *Columbia Journalism Review* article about this episode included the headline, "No story is so good that it doesn't have to be checked."[2]

(While the expose on the use of the plane misfired, Governor Mandel was convicted in mid-1977 of fraud and racketeering because of his involvement in the secret purchase of a horseracing track. Apparently, the *Sun* had the right instincts if not the right facts in the airplane case. But that is all the more reason to be accurate in reporting.)

The newsroom adage Never Check Out a Good Story is generally said with tongue in cheek. When it is followed, it is usually because a reporter is so confident he is correct that a double check is not needed. The reporter knows the answers, so he does not bother to ask questions—until it is too late. Another example should make the point clear.

An Albany, New York, killing was called a "torture slaying" by the newspapers because the victim had been cut and the killer apparently applied a hot knife to parts of the victim's body, causing burns and slashes. After four or five days of big headlines, the story died down. There were no leads, no more suspects. Then another body was found. The corpse appeared cut. The "torture slayer" had struck again. At least in the morning newspaper the slayer had struck. In the afternoon paper it was reported that the victim had died of natural causes, and because the body was not found right away some skin fissures developed in the normal process of decay. A morning paper's reporter, under the pressures of deadline and given the opportunity to resurrect a readable story, had not asked the coroner about the cause of death! Small wonder one might be moved to applaud when a reporter asks the necessary question.

The discussion so far has offered some anecdotes and a few observations as to why it is often difficult to ask good questions. You might get the impression that once a good question is framed, the problems are solved and the reporter has the story. Not quite. Remember our second assumption at the start: How a reporter gathers information determines what information from his news source ultimately reaches the news media audience. Consider just three different ways reporters gather information through interviews: by telephone, by face-to-face conversation, by press conferences. Each method of gathering news is likely to produce a different story or at least is more suitable for some stories than for others. Each has advantages and disadvantages.

It is easy to list the advantages of the telephone. In fact Professor Eugene Webb of Stanford, author of at least two works of value to reporters,[3] despaired of overreliance on the telephone and joked that a book about information-gathering techniques used by reporters would need only two chapters. The first would be "The Telephone"; the second, "Everything Else."

If one has very specific questions to ask, use of the telephone cannot be beaten. It is fast and inexpensive in covering the so-called routine news—making the rounds of police and fire departments, getting the day's high and low temperatures, determining the date and time of a city council meeting, obtaining the details on how one licenses a dog. One can cover considerable distance in a short time by using the phone. Additionally people nowadays seem to have more time for a telephone call than for meeting with others in person, partly because a phone call may be presumed to take up less time than a face-to-face meeting.

Many reporters, upon being told by a secretary that "Mr. Hinkley cannot see you now," have just walked down the hall and telephoned him to get the information they wanted. The more bizarre episodes of this nature involve reporters who telephone a bank to talk with the bank robbers while the robbery is in process, or telephone criminals in a house in which the residents are held hostage. No matter how busy a person is, there often is time for a short telephone call.

Another advantage of the telephone is that it permits the reporter to take notes without distracting the news source. Nor is the news source distracted by the reporter's clothes, breath, or general physical appearance. Further, the impersonal nature of a telephone conversation may allow the reporter to ask more pointed questions than he or she might ask in person. In a telephone exchange, the worst the news source can immediately do is to hang up. In face-to-face meeting, a reporter might not want to ask a pointed question and risk "the worst the other person can do."

With the telephone second and third call-backs for additional information are not uncommon, but traipsing back to a news source's office or residence for the second or third time is likely to become unproductive or at least too time consuming.

One final advantage: the reporter also may have the assistance of a good telephone operator, employed by the news medium or by the phone company. A good telephone operator may be as dedicated to finding a news source for a reporter as a good librarian is to finding the book a reader wants. A reporter who antagonizes phone operators reduces his or her reporting potential considerably.

A discussion of the telephone must include reference to the late Harry Romanoff, a Chicago newspaperman known to some as "the Heifetz of the telephone" because of his inventive but often unethical use of the phone to gather news. Romanoff's forte was impersonating public officials and others via telephone to get information that a news source would not normally give to reporters. At the time of the 1966 mass murder of eight nursing students in Chicago, Romanoff pretended to be the Cook County coroner and elicited from a policeman, over the phone, the details of the slayings. Then he talked to the mother of suspect Richard Speck by pretending to be her son's attorney. Once—the story goes—Romanoff phoned a crime scene and, identifying himself as the coroner, demanded information about the murder. He found himself talking to the real coroner.

This bring us to disadvantages of using the telephone. For one thing, a news source can talk on only one telephone at a time. For a reporter anxious to contact a news source, one thing as bad as no answer to a phone call is to receive a busy signal, suggesting that the news source probably is there and maybe even talking to another reporter. All the reporter can do is hang up and try again.

When the reporter does get through, he or she does not know many things about the telephone news source. Is the news source alone, or are others in the room listening to and affecting what he says? Is the news source silently smirking when he gives what sound like straight-faced answers? It has happened.

A newspaper reporter was at the Tulare County, California, sheriff's office getting information on a drowning from an irascible deputy sheriff, Jim Fluty. As Fluty gave the reporter the written report on the drowning, the telephone rang. It was someone from a local radio station, making the rounds of his news sources. All the newspaper reporter could hear, as he read a deputy's report of the drowning, was Fluty's end of the conversation. It went something like this:

> "Well, it has been pretty quiet. No traffic fatals.
> "No, there haven't been any burglaries.
> "No, there haven't been any robberies.
> "No, no rapes or murders.
> "No, no fires that I know of.
> "No, no serious traffic accidents.
> "No, no assaults.
> "Yes, I guess it has been pretty quiet. Anything else? Goodbye."

Jim Fluty smiled.

Lessons like that are not lost on young reporters, and maybe the lesson was not lost when the radio station newsman learned much later about the drowning. Fluty would of course protest that he had been honest in all his responses to the telephone questions.

Specificity was listed as an advantage of using the phone; if one wants specific information, it is easy to get by phone. Yet the time constraints on phone calls may limit the number of topics a reporter can cover. If something unexpected comes up, or if a reporter wants to pursue some new information, there may not be the time to do so over the phone.

The telephone often is simply not useful in chasing fast-breaking news or other newsworthy events. News—by some of its definitions—is the unexpected, the unassumed, the surprising. And the unexpected, the unassumed, and the surprising do not always occur next to phone booths—despite the ease with which reporter Clark Kent managed to find phone booths for his change in roles to Superman.

The relatively recent interest in nonverbal communication and body language[4] suggests another shortcoming of the telephone. In a phone interview there is almost a complete absence of nonverbal information the reporter might find useful in interpreting the news source's responses and in providing the news audience with more accurate information. The only nonverbal information available to a reporter by telephone is time—the pauses in a news source's answers. Beyond that the reporter has not the slightest idea as to the news source's demeanor and has no picture of facial expressions, body movements, and hand gestures to pass along to the reader.

One last telephone disadvantage worth listing is that it is easier for the news source to terminate the questioning by abruptly hanging up, accidentally cutting off the reporter, or hurriedly saying, "I'm sorry, I have to go now, goodbye." Any of these is easier than ushering a reporter out or walking away from those often dubbed "newshounds."

Use of the telephone, then, is not much different from use of any other tool: it is well suited for certain tasks, but if one uses it indiscriminately there are problems.

The same can be said of the in-person interviews, and there are advantages and disadvantages in working with a news source face to face. Face to face the reporter gets considerably more time to cover new areas that come up during the conversation; the news source's remarks are seen in context because the reporter is dealing with the news source in the source's surroundings and not with an impersonal voice over the phone; it is more difficult for the news source to terminate the conversation; the news source can make his or her points clearer by drawing charts or pointing out visual evidence to the reporter; the reporter may be able to develop better rapport with the news source by investing the time and energy needed to see someone in person (indeed a reporter usually is well advised to occasionally visit in person those news sources usually contacted by phone); news sources may be reached "live" at a news event more readily than they can be reached by phone.

The disadvantages are few but important. Personal interviews may consume more time and more money, and both commodities may be scarce. A considerable amount of the information exchanged in a face-to-face encounter—social amenities such as talking about the weather, expressing congratulations or sympathy—is time consuming and does not yield much if anything in the way of newsworthy material.

While seeing someone in person might enable a reporter to establish better rapport than is possible by phone, more problems might arise in the encounter. The news source may be at least distracted and at worst antagonized by the reporter's notetaking, physical appearance, facial gestures, or other mannerisms beyond the reporter's control or consciousness. A reporter's overreliance on the telephone is poor conditioning for face-to-face encounters. On the telephone one can smile, frown, blink, yawn, close one's eyes, or raise one's eyebrows without the news source's ever knowing it. The same twitches may have a damning effect on a face-to-face interview.

It was not overreliance on the telephone that caused problems when Louis Rukeyser tried to interview economic commentator Eliot Janeway on the television program *Wall Street Week*. But their verbal sparring on that program illustrates the problems that arise when a news source and a reporter generate more heat than light for the audience. Rukeyser sought to discuss Janeway's predictions that the Dow-Jones industrial average might drop a couple hundred points to 425. He did not get off to a good start when he labeled Janeway "one of America's most persistent forecasters of doom," but Janeway was interrupting him even before Rukeyser could say—as he intended to—that Janeway did not like to be called a prophet of doom.

From there on the viewer got little additional information. Here is a brief excerpt from the program:

RUKEYSER: More, more than five years ago you were talking about 425. Just over four . . . let me just finish the question please. Just over four years ago . . .
JANEWAY: You're not, you're not, you're not asking a question.
RUKEYSER: I will . . .
JANEWAY: You're making a statement. . . . You're talking about an interview with me in the *New York Times* by Vartan. . . .
RUKEYSER: No, I'm talking about a radio program you and I were on in '69, and just over four years ago on this very program, you predicted an imminent market collapse. . . .
JANEWAY: Yes.
RUKEYSER: And just the opposite happened.
JANEWAY: Oh. What is . . .
RUKEYSER: And this past winter . . . this past winter . . .
JANEWAY: . . . wait a minute . . . what is true? . . .
RUKEYSER: Could I just ask the question?
JANEWAY: No, you . . . because what you think you are . . .
RUKEYSER: Let me . . .
JANEWAY: . . . is a road company Joe McCarthy . . . . he really was a big league inquisitor compared to your simplistic shabbiness.
RUKEYSER: I'm just quoting your prediction.
JANEWAY: Now slow down.

And so it went, until at the end of the program Rukeyser noted, "In five years of programing, this is the fewest questions we've ever gotten to ask, which I think may speak for itself."[5]

It is doubtful that the Rukeyser–Janeway quarrel could have been avoided even if Louis Rukeyser had a handy list of "things to do to put the person being interviewed at ease." Rukeyser acknowledged that the program did not yield much substantive information for the viewer. Such honest assessments do not always follow a third form of interviewing—the press conference.

It is difficult to think of any worthwhile advantage the press conference has for the competent news reporter. It may be that this is one of the reasons for the use of the press conference by public officials and private entrepeneurs whose development of the press conference has helpd give rise to the phrase "pseudo event"—an event contrived to create news interest where none exists or is merited.

One value of the news conference by a public official is the symbolic nature of the event, and perhaps this is reason enough to continue the practice. At a press conference in this nation, a public official supposedly opens himself to examination by responding to unsolicited and perhaps even antagonistic questions.

One advantage to the reporter is that the press conference may allow access to a public official. An advantage to some reporters is that they can simply sit, listen, and take notes while other reporters do the work of asking questions. But most of the other advantages lie with the news source: he generally decides who asks questions; he determines the length of the answers; he can deny anyone the right to ask a follow-up question; he often sets the time, place, and duration of the interview; he can easily rephrase tough questions to his liking.

The press conference more than the telephone or face-to-face interview makes it difficult for the reporter to get worthwhile information, because the press conference makes the two assumptions of this chapter irrelevant. We assumed that if a reporter prepared and asked good questions, he or she might get a better story. But at a press conference, particularly one of size, the well-prepared reporter may never get to ask a question—indeed may be avoided as a troublemaker—and certainly is unlikely to have a chance to ask a follow-up question if the first is ill-answered. Our second assumption recognizes the link between how information is gathered and what information is gathered. The press conference stacks the deck against the reporter in favor of the news source.

It is time now to consider what the reporter can do in newsgathering situations to stack the deck more in his or her favor—more precisely, to stack the deck in favor of getting worthwhile information for his reader, viewer, or listener. Keeping in mind the warnings about relying on gimmicks or devices to produce newsworthy information, a reporter can still do some things to help assure that the news reporter–news source relationship works to the advantage of the news media audience. Let us limit the discussion of what the reporter can do to three areas: preparation, awareness of the competence of the news source, and the nature of the questions.

PREPARATION

Washington Post reporter and columnist David S. Broder is said to have the "reputation of a reporter who does his homework."[6] That is a deserved accolade for the respected Mr. Broder. But if one thinks about it, the compliment is an indictment of hundreds of other reporters. What is said to set Broder and similar skilled reporters apart is that they study and prepare before doing their stories and columns. Unfortunately, it probably is true that what sets many good reporters apart from their less competent peers is that the better reporters care enough about what they are doing to "do their homework."

The nature of much of news coverage requires reporters to be well read on contemporary events. Like other professionals and craftsmen, the reporter must keep up to date on his or her subject matter; the difference for the reporter is that the subject matter is—in the broadest of terms—"the human condition." While that subject is too broad, there is the advantage that a great deal of what a reporter reads or witnesses will—at one time or another—help in coverage of the news.

To get down to specifics, a reporter can take advantage of his newspaper's library, a public library, and current periodicals for a quick refresher course on topics ranging from NATO to sewage treatment. Some preparation is better than none, and a little preparation is far more than many reporters ever have. Probably no investment pays as much dividend as a little research by a reporter. Many news sources have dedicated a good part of their lives to their vocations or other areas of interest and activity which they are asked to share with the reporter. Knowledge the reporter can demonstrate about that area of interest often makes the news source more responsive to questions—if only because many news sources have encountered so many other people, including reporters, who haven't evidenced the slightest interest in the news source's area of expertise.

Preparation can save time. Knowing the news source's background, the reporter can move on from there and dwell on questions that will yield newsworthy material rather than simply informing the reporter about the news source's age and education.

Even a modest bit of preparation is useful in placing a news source's comments in perspective. On *Meet the Press*, Los Angeles Police Chief Edward M. Davis spoke against gun control. In response to a question from columnist James J. Kilpatrick, Davis said only 3 percent of crimes involved handguns and therefore any effect of gun control laws on crime would be miniscule. Kilpatrick pointed out that the 3 percent figure was misleading because guns were not used in car thefts, larceny, and many other crimes. Kilpatrick added that about 53 percent of the 20,000 homicides in the nation each year involved handguns.[7] It was just a minor exchange of points of view, but the viewer had more information—thanks to Kilpatrick's preparation and questioning—than if Davis's response had stood unclarified.

If a reporter is to interview a person about a subject such as strip mining, obviously the reporter should read about strip mining before talking to the news source. If a reporter is to interview a news source for a personality sketch, the reporter should study the background of the news source before talking with him or her.

Consider an interview with the late singer and movie star Ethel Waters. In her autobiography *His Eye Is on the Sparrow* she disclosed that she was conceived when her mother was raped at knife-point by Johnny Waters. That sort of information helped one better understand Ethel Waters, but it was not information likely to be uncovered in a brief interview.

THE COMPETENCE OF THE NEWS SOURCE

Being prepared for an interview includes giving some thought to the competence of the news source. Much reporting would be improved if reporters would frequently ask themselves: What is this news source competent to talk about? What can this news source tell me and my readers that few others can?

When Neil Armstrong was about to become the first person to set foot on the surface of the moon, a television reporter was at the home of Armstrong's parents in Wapakoneta, Ohio, and had the opportunity to interview them on network television. What question do you ask the mother of the first man to step on the moon? What particular "news" or insights can she give you? You might ask, "As Neil is about to step on the moon, what thoughts, what memories of his childhood do you find yourself thinking about?" or "What thoughts of his childhood are most dear to you?" Such questions would give Mrs. Armstrong an opportunity to give an answer only she could give. Such questions might also provide very interesting, perhaps moving, answers for the television viewer or newspaper reader.

Instead, however, the television newsman asked Mrs. Armstrong something to this effect: "What do you think the chances are for a successful mission?" And Neil's father was asked,

"What do you think the Russians are doing up there?" (At that time Russia also had launched a lunar space shot.) The answers from Mr. and Mrs. Armstrong were understandably awkward and somewhat predictable. They had faith in the engineers and scientists who would send their son to the moon and bring him back, and they were not sure what the Russians were up to, if anything. But that was it. Failure to ask good questions had produced poor, almost useless answers, particularly when the parents could have added a poignant moment to the moonshot coverage.

Good questions will encourage or permit the news source to tell the reporter what he thinks and not what he thinks the reporter or others want to hear. Good questions also may help the reporter avoid some of the stereotyped or predictable answers that news sources may give as a matter of habit. The challenge confronting the reporter is not only to consider what the news source is competent to comment on but also to seek possible new approaches to the news source's area of competence. Many news sources have been interviewed so much that they know what questions to expect, and their responses are practiced and automatic.

Upon being introduced to a young reporter, comedian Jimmy Durante dictated the story:

"Okay, kid, here's what you do. You start off with this quote." Durante furnished the quote. Then Durante dictated the rest of the story to the reporter and said, "Then you end it with this quote." Again Durante furnished the quote.

The reporter wrote the story just as Durante had dictated it, because the episode caught the flavor of Durante and offered insights to the man that were difficult to handle any other way.

On a less heavy handed basis many sources do the same thing to reporters. The challenge to the reporter often is to get the news source to consider some new approaches to what seems an old subject. When that occurs, the news source may have a refreshing experience; the reporter has a better story; and the reader, viewer, or listener is treated to information previously unreported.

In considering the competence of the news source, the reporter should keep in mind not only the news source's area of expertise but also what manner of interviewing is most likely to produce the desired information. Perhaps some information is best obtained by reading articles the source has written; perhaps other information is better obtained by talking to the news source's friends or critics; perhaps some information is best obtained by merely observing and not asking any questions at all.

Some of the most misleading advice that can be given to reporters is that "kids say the darnedest things." Television personality Art Linkletter made that saying popular because of the cute and clever things children would say on his shows. Yet reporters who have interviewed children find that common responses to their questions are "I don't know," "I guess so," or "Fine." It is in doing stories on children that a reporter's powers of observation are more useful than merely asking questions. If you want to know how handicapped children enjoy a trip to the zoo, you don't ask them; you watch them.

THE NATURE OF THE QUESTIONS

It sounded like an interesting news item, as the television reporter began, "Democratic and Republican Congressmen have accused each other of foot-dragging on the issue of . . ." The newsman gave additional information about the charges of foot-dragging. Then the viewer saw the reporter interviewing a Democratic House leader. Question: "Do you think the Republicans have been foot-dragging on this issue?" As one might safely predict, the Democrat did not pass up the opportunity to agree that the GOP has been foot-dragging.

The next sequence showed the newsman talking to a Republican. Question: "Do you think the Democrats have been foot-dragging on this issue?"

By that time it was clear that what had started out as a news item about who was to blame for lack of Congressional action was more of a pseudo event resulting from the reporter's question. Is it really newsworthy that, given the chance to agree or disagree that the opposition is at fault, politicians are likely to agree that the opposition has—in this case—been foot-dragging?

It is not always as obvious as it was in the "foot-dragging" episode, but often how a reporter phrases his question determines what answer he will get. A few things can safely be said about asking questions:

1. When we respond to questions, generally we are aware of what the person asking us wants to hear; more often than not we are likely to tell that person not what we think but what we think he wants to hear.

2. Often questions are asked in such sweeping terms that the respondent can say virtually anything and still—as the saying goes—be in the ballpark. (How do you feel about war?) This makes it most difficult to compare answers from different sources.

3. Many questions ask the respondent to make hypothetical and unrealistic choices.

The reporter's task is to avoid these and other pitfalls in gathering information from news sources. How can a reporter do this? One way is to avoid asking questions that call for only a negative or only a positive response. Ask the news source questions that provide an opportunity for either or both. Instead of asking, "What do you see as problems caused by busing of school children?" a reporter might ask, "What do you see as the arguments for and against beginning the busing of school children in this community this fall?" The first question limits the respondent to a negative answer; the second question permits both positive and negative responses and also specifies the exact time and place the respondent is to consider in his response. Some research in the behavioral sciences suggests that respondents are likely to be more honest in their criticisms if they are also given the opportunity to say something positive about the subject they are criticizing.

When asking "either-or" questions, the reporter should recognize that there may be a number of other alternatives available to the respondent. We ask respondents if they will vote for a Democratic or Republican candidate and rule out countless other possibilities, including whether they will vote at all.

In their discussion on interviewing, Webb and Salancik cite impressive research suggesting ways reporters can improve the questions they ask:

1. Avoid words with a double meaning. Equivocal and vague wording of questions, use of emotionally charged terms, and reporters' statements in the guise of questions are of little use in eliciting newsworthy material from a source.

2. Avoid long questions.

3. Specify exactly the time, place, and context you want the respondent to assume. If you want a news source to comment on the general philosophy of government regulation of advertising, say so.

4. Either make explicit all the alternatives the respondent

should have in mind when he answers, or make none of them explicit. Do not lead the news source by suggesting a desired answer and not mentioning other alternatives open to him.

5. It is often helpful to ask questions in terms of the respondent's own immediate and recent experience rather than in terms of generalities.[8]

Finally reporters should remember that follow-up questions often are needed and almost always are helpful. Perhaps the news source really does not answer the first question; perhaps the answer raises other questions.

A reporter may not be able to anticipate all the questions that have to be asked. But if there are good initial questions, it will be easier to pose the second and third questions that begin to put the issue in perspective for the reporter and the news audience. The better the questions in quality and in quantity, the better check the reporter develops on his news source's competence and credibility. In asking good questions, the reporter not only gathers better information for the news audience but also can better test the news source.

Recommended Readings
Newman, Robert P., and Newman, Dale R. *Evidence*. Boston: Houghton Mifflin Company, 1969.
Rivers, William L. *Finding Facts*. Englewood Cliffs, N.J.: Prentice-Hall, 1975.
Webb, Eugene J., and Salancik, Jerry R. *The Interview or the Only Wheel in Town*, Journalism Monograph No. 2, 1966. See bibliography, pp. 41–49.
Webb, Eugene J. et al. *Unobstrusive Measures: Nonreactive Research in the Social Sciences*. Chicago: Rand McNally & Company, 1966. See bibliography, pp. 187–215.

4 | Informing, protecting, and promoting news sources

Here are three interesting perspectives on the role of the reporter in our society.

Ben Hecht—reporter, playwright, novelist—wrote of himself as a young reporter in Chicago in the early 1900s.

> He knew almost nothing. His achievements were nil.
> He was as void of ambition as an eel is of feathers.
> He misunderstood himself and the world around him.
> He thought journalism was some sort of game like
> stoop-tag. He was a pauper without troubles or prob-
> lems. He was as in love with life as an ant on a sum-
> mer blade of grass.[1]

Roy Fisher, editor of the *Chicago Daily News* before becoming dean of the School of Journalism at the University of
Missouri, took a broader and more sobering view of what reporters and the news media do in our society in the 1970s.

> It is the mass media, these that serve society across
> the board, that give a mob the capacity to become a
> society, and a society the capacity to be free.[2]

Professor William Rivers of Stanford University, who has written about as much as anyone on the role of the reporter in society, noted:

> The stickiest problem in journalism is defining the proper stance of the reporter toward his source.[3]

Ben Hecht's likening of the journalism of his era to a game of stoop-tag—with combinations of mayhem, malarky, and madcap adventures—probably is almost as accurate as it is enticing. News sources were foils who existed primarily to enable the reporter to do a more clever job of reporting. One or two quotes from the source were proof that the reporter did not make up *everything.* But the innocence and immaturity that allowed a young nation to indulge reporters such as Ben Hecht was lost, as Hecht himself noted,[4] during World War I.

The relationship between the reporter and news source is now complex, as suggested by Dean Fisher's comment. The desired result of a news story nowadays is not necessarily enhancement of a reporter's ego and entertainment of an audience. Reporters and the news audience now take themselves and each other more seriously—for better or for worse.

Journalism reviews, spawned in the aftermath of the Democratic National Convention in Chicago in 1968, criticize the media for inaccuracies in reporting that are child's play compared to the shenanigans of Hecht's generation. Television programs such as *Meet the Press, Issues and Answers,* and *Firing Line* and columnists by the score are evidence that the media pay more than lip service to the idea that our system of government requires an informed electorate capable of self-rule.

The Watergate period of American history and the resignation of President Nixon symbolize perhaps better than anything else the emergence of a news industry credited with powerful influence, somewhat adjusted to a high degree of introspection, and placed under increasing scrutiny by the audience and government officials.

When Rivers writes of newsmen and public officials as "adversaries" or Fisher discusses the relationship between the mass media and a free society, their comments reflect changes in society, changes in the media, and changes in the reporter and the perception of the reporter's role. The stance of the reporter toward his or her sources—what Rivers called "the stickiest problem"—is a decidedly contemporary issue.

The serving of subpoenas on reporters, shield laws, jail sentences, police masquerading as newsmen, cloaked attribution in news stories—all these are part of the question of reporters' relationships with their news sources. Our concerns with these relationships are (1) How do they affect what we have termed newsgathering as part of the power of the press? (2) How do they affect what ultimately reaches news consumers?

This chapter will consider these relationships in only three ways—as the reporter *informs* news sources, *protects* news sources, and *promotes* news sources. Perhaps what follows will leave one hungering for the halcyon days when a reporter had no troubles and no problems and "was as in love with life as an ant on a summer blade of grass." Well, those days are not gone forever. Newsgathering continues to be exciting and enjoyable. But it is also more complex, partly because society now demands more of the reporter and reporters demand more of themselves. No easy answers are offered, but our survey of reporter—news source relationships may suggest what some of the questions are.

INFORMING NEWS SOURCES

Sometimes it comes as a shock to a reporter when he or she must tell a news source something the source was presumed to know:

In a boating accident off the California coast, a man drowns and several others are injured. Hours later a

> reporter for an inland paper phones the home of the drowning victim, mentally prepared for the person answering the phone to be upset and perhaps inaudible.

If the victim's family is too upset, maybe a neighbor or a cousin will be at home and I can get the information from one of them, the reporter thinks. The reporter, however, is greeted by a cheery "Hello"; instead of getting information about the victim, it is the reporter who breaks the news of the accident to the family and provides a coastal phone number to call for further information.

> The crash of a private plane in another state kills a local woman. The reporter reads the Associated Press story about the crash and then phones the victim's home for additional information.

But he does not get the information, because no one at the home knew about the accident until the newsman phoned. Understandably, the reporter is asked to please phone back later.

These instances are dramatic illustrations of the role of the reporter in providing information to people presumed to be news sources.

The exchange of roles, as in news about death,[5] is readily apparent and uncomfortable for the reporter. Accustomed to gathering information and transmitting that information to an impersonal news audience, the reporter suddenly becomes the news source providing information to people who are supposed to tell him what has happened. Aren't they? Isn't that what reporting is all about?

No, not really. Reporters often disclose their opinions, views, and expectations inadvertently, as discussed in the preceding chapter. And sometimes reporters share information not so inadvertently. With increasing emphasis on specialized reporting, newsmen may even become valued sources of information for public officials seeking solutions to difficult problems.

Donald Bolles, an investigative reporter for the *Phoenix Arizona Republic,* was killed in June 1976 by a bomb rigged to his car. Presumably Bolles knew too much about land fraud schemes in Arizona. Four years earlier he had testified before the Select Committee on Crime of the U.S. House of Representatives. His reporting had made him an expert on ties among the Emprise Corporation of Buffalo, New York, organized crime, and dog racing in Arizona.

James Risser of the *Des Moines Register* did not testify before Congress, but he was recognized for his knowledge about corruption in the grain export trade. Risser, who won the Pulitzer Prize for national reporting in 1976 for his expose of that corruption, admitted that he felt uneasy when congressmen asked his opinion on pending legislation and other proposals to combat grain trade corruption. He was uneasy because of what he saw as the danger of his becoming a participant in a news story he was covering. His solution, in part, was to discuss alternatives open to Congress and share insights with the public officials but to stop well short of advocating public policy to those who were his news sources.

Bolles and Risser had at least two advantages not always available to reporters working with news sources: they knew the people they were talking with were seeking information that might be used at a later time; they had options as to whether they would answer questions and, if so, to what extent they would provide the information and opinions desired.

However, as the court records of recent years indicate, reporters sometimes are asked for information under threat of being jailed if they do not comply with a court order. The specialization of reporters and the access of many of them to dissident groups in society have made it tempting for grand juries, attorneys general, police, and other public officials to seek information from reporters through subpoena, contempt proceedings, or other legal avenues.

The new definitions of newsman—news source relationships, sometimes forced upon reporters, are both symbol and sign of the changing role of reporters in our society.

In the spring of 1973 an Associated Press photographer, James Mone, chatted with FBI agents after taking some pictures during the Indian occupation of Wounded Knee, South Dakota. A year later, Mone was fired by the AP because he "acted improperly as an impartial newsman." The president and general manager of AP, Wes Gallagher, said, "It is against AP policy for any AP man to be involved in any way in any news story."[6]

That is a strict policy. Mone saw his chats with the FBI as

little more than passing the time of day and as facilitating his work as a newsman: "If we tell them [the FBI] something that really isn't anything new, they get the idea they have somebody to talk to and they'll keep the door open to Wounded Knee [so reporters can continue to go there]."[7]

Mone had given the agents an estimate of the number of persons and weapons in the occupied village. But, in the course of his work, Mone also talked with the Indian leaders, giving them what he considered safe information. For example, Mone said he told Dennis Banks and Russell Means that about an hour after the government denied there were armored personnel carriers in Martin, South Dakota, Mone took photos of more than 20 such vehicles in Martin.

While much of the information Mone shared with the Indian leaders and FBI agents was reported in the newspapers, an FBI report listed Mone as a "protected confidential source." Mone had asked that his name not be in reports since he did not want to testify in court. When Mone was identified as an FBI source a year later, he was suspended and then fired, because he refused to resign, for violating the AP policy on becoming involved in a news story.

The AP policy if followed literally would decimate AP ranks around the nation and the forces of other news media as well. Reporters are involved in stories by the mere fact of coverage; the manner in which the reporter covers the event often shapes the news that reaches the public. The better test is not involvement "in any way" but competence of the reporter in observing and reporting an issue in sensitive fashion, limiting as best he or she can intrusion into the news event as it unfolds.

What the AP and other news agencies are concerned about is the reporter's role becoming secondary to other interests. For example, Jacque Srouji was fired by the *Nashville Tennessean* in Spring 1976 because the paper was convinced she used her news job to provide the FBI with information about dissidents and perhaps about professional colleagues as well.

The reporter's role as an intermediary of news sources seldom has been etched as starkly as when Tom Wicker of the *New York Times* went to Attica Prison in upstate New York in 1971. Wicker was one of several persons whom rebellious prisoners invited to Attica to negotiate between them and prison authorities for a resolution to the convicts' grievances and an end to the prison unrest. Wicker tells of that painful episode in his reporting career in the book *A Time to Die* (Quadrangle/New York Times); 43 persons were killed, all but one by lawmen's gunfire, when the negotiations failed and the prison yard was recaptured by force.

Wicker's visibility as an intermediary at Attica seemed to preclude any misuse or abuse of his role as a reporter. Readers were forewarned of his involvement. More often than not, however, the reporter's role as an intermediary or a source of information can be characterized by such words as *involuntary, subtle,* and *inadvertent.*

One of the points stressed in the preceding chapter was that information or attitudes passed on to a news source inadvertently or unintentionally may be as effective in shaping the news story as information transmitted in heavy-handed or conspiratorial fashion. Again there are no easy answers. A reporter must at times share information with news sources—educate them, if you will—to get a more informed response to questions that should be answered for the public. The reporter is not a mere transmission belt, taking information from one source and passing it along to another. Rather the reporter is a participant in an important and complex communication process. If the reporter is sensitive to how he or she influences what happens in that process, the news audience will be better served.

PROTECTING NEWS SOURCES

A reporter might protect a news source by defending the source's credibility and reputation or by keeping the source's identity secret. A reporter might do these things for selfish reasons, e.g., to fend off challenges to his own competence and judgment in quoting that source; he might protect the news source at the request of the source; or he might protect the source for the benefit of the news audience. Of these various possibilities, protection for the benefit of the news audience will be of the most concern to us. But let us first consider the other reasons.

To Aid the Reporter

It is a cliche that a reporter often is only as good as his news sources. Certainly a reporter is of little use to an employer or the news audience if the sources he or she frequently relies on are inaccurate, self-serving, misleading, or irrelevant. Because of the way newspapers are read and broadcasts are listened to, it is the *St. Louis Post-Dispatch* that the reader thinks is in error, not the news sources; it is CBS, NBC, or ABC that the listener thinks is wrong, not the news sources.

Reporters turning in questionable or controversial stories may be questioned by copy editors or news editors as to the veracity of the news sources. It is a twofold test: Can the news source be trusted? Is the reporter discerning enough to know when a usually reliable source might be misleading?

The reporter's assessment of the news source is important because the media can be manipulated to serve the source; if a story is at all controversial, there are likely to be many other "reliable news sources" with other points of view. Their opinions will be reported too, and perhaps given more emphasis by competing media.

If a story must be modified, clarified, or corrected because a news source was off base, the reporter may be considered less useful for having news sources that cannot be trusted or for not being able to discern when he or she is being misled. Because a reporter at times has such a stake in the reliability of a news source, there may be a temptation or tendency to support that source—in the newsroom and in public print—by giving less emphasis to contrary points of view, even when evidence begins to build that the source is wrong this time. At its worst, such an approach puts short-term advantages—maintaining as best one can the reputation of the paper, reporter, and news source—ahead of the long-term credibility of the paper and responsibility to the news audience.

To Aid the News Source

News sources might seek the protection or support of the reporter in a number of ways: they might ask to review a story before it is published or broadcast; they might request that certain comments not be reported; they might request anonymity.

It is common on the high school and college level, and not uncommon in the commercial press, for news sources to request to see a story before it is written or even to refuse to comment unless such assurances are given. In making such requests, the news sources often say they want to see the story only "in the interests of accuracy." In most newsrooms, however, there is strong peer group pressure to discourage reporters from complying with such requests. Reasons for such pressure include at least the following:

1. Professional competence: If the professional reporter cannot interview people and observe events and report his or her observations faithfully, perhaps that person should not be a reporter after all. The reporter cannot and should not escape the burden of responsibility for what he or she reports. A reporter should accept and recognize that responsibility and not attempt to escape the burden by having news sources check the stories.

2. Fairness: Going back to a news source for his or her approval may be inequitable and unfair unless the reporter can do so for all news sources; this may be impractical, may lend itself to prejudicial behavior by the reporter, or may be ill-advised for the reasons above and below.

3. Purpose: The reporter's purpose is different from the news source's. The reporter's purpose is not primarily or even secondarily to put the news source in the best possible light. Yet this is what the news source may intend to do in pre-publication review of a story.

4. Access to information: In some cases, particularly those involving public agencies or public officials, a request for pre-publication review of an article is inconsistent with the rights all citizens have of access to and use of public information.

5. Pressures of time: News agencies do business *today,* and it seems to border on folly for a supposedly competent news operation to be delayed while a news source checks a story to make sure it is "correct."

The above points do *not* mean that the reporter should not check back on things he or she is unclear about or may not have understood. The reporter should check back frequently and repeatedly with a news source if there is any question about the accuracy of a news item.

News sources might also request that some comments not be reported, saying the comments are "off the record." Two points are worth making here: (1) Sometimes requests for keeping comments "off the record" are made at public meetings or in the presence of dozens of other persons. In such cases the comments cannot be off the record, and the source should be so informed. The news audience has as much right to the information as those in attendance. (2) When a source requests that some material be off the record and the reporter agrees, it should be clear to both reporter and news source precisely what information is off the record—for background purposes only. It may not be unusual for a news source to talk along and have some information on the record and some off, leaving the reporter confused as to which notes are usable for the news story and which are not.

A news source at times may say something that he or she suddenly realizes should not have been said. Then the source may request the news media not to report the comment. During a legislative session, an Iowa state legislator referred to some people as "working like niggers." He immediately said he did not mean what he had said. The comments should not be interpreted as racist and he would appreciate it if the news media would not report the comment, he said. The Des Moines paper did report the comment, along with the legislator's explanation and plea for nonpublication. The comment was made at a public meeting by an elected official, whose disclaimer also was reported. There simply was no compelling reason not to report what he said.

Sometimes the language of public officials or of people who write letters to the editor is "cleaned up" by reporters or copy editors to rid it of vulgarities or grammatical errors. Laundering of such language is not necessarily to protect the news source. Generally the reasoning is that the news source's comment is made easier for readers to understand or that the news audience would object strongly to the use of the original language.

Discussions about whether to print comments by a public official probably peaked in Fall 1976 when Secretary of Agriculture Earl A. Butz was identified as the Ford cabinet member who uttered the gross explanation as to why the GOP would not get the Negro vote. Few papers published the comments word for word. Here is how it appeared in the *Des Moines Register* during the turmoil which led to Butz's resignation in early October.

> I'll tell you why you can't attract coloreds. Because coloreds only want three things. You know what they want? I'll tell you what coloreds want; it's three

> things: First a tight (obscenity); second, loose shoes; and third, a warm place to (vulgarism).

Then the paper added: "The obscenity was a sexual term; the vulgarism an excretory term."

Michael Gartner, editor of the *Register* and *Tribune,* gave a logical explanation for the way his papers reported the episode, and it's also why the direct quote doesn't appear here.

> Butz was as gross as a human can be. By printing blanks we did not leave open the possibility that the reader would assume Butz said something worse than he actually uttered. . . . What's more, here the thought was more important than the words, and the quoted material leaves no doubt that, as the (Washington) *Post* editorialized, Butz thinks blacks are animals.
>
> The lesson in all of this seems to be that if an important person swears mildly to make an important point, we'll print it. We'll print it because it's probably not offensive to most, and we might be doing the speaker a disservice by implying he was cruder than he in fact was.
>
> But if an important person is especially gross in making an important point, we won't print it. It's offensive, and bowdlerizing would not lead to unfair inference.[8]

The debate over publishing vulgarities is a continuing one. The people and the circumstances change, but the question remains the same: When do you launder language?

When vulgarities are left in a story, it is because they are thought to be germane. Consider a case less celebrated than that involving Butz: this episode involved Antonio G. (Tony) Felicetta, who was appointed to the Minneapolis Human Rights Commission in 1969 by Mayor Charles Stenvig.

In a *Minneapolis Tribune* story that began on page one, Felicetta was introduced to the readers under the headline "Public Official Speaks His Mind."[9] The lead paragraph was: "Antonio G. (Tony) Felicetta doesn't mince words. He mauls them." In the fourth and fifth paragraphs, the reporter began acquainting the reader with Felicetta's philosophy for his place on the human relations commission:

> "I'm not going to take any bullshit," he said speaking of intimidation by some blacks and Indians

he said has occurred at meetings of the Human Relations Commission and elsewhere.

"If there are any grievances," he said, "I sure as hell would want to see them taken care of. But I sure as hell wouldn't want to give 'em half my paycheck when I'm working and they're sitting on their asses."

After describing Felicetta and his participation in such civic activities as raising money for amateur and professional sports as well as for the March of Dimes and the American Cancer Society, the 30-paragraph story concluded with these two paragraphs:

But Felicetta emphasized that he's not against minority people, he's just against "the 30 or so who are causing all the trouble . . . 98 percent of the colored people in this city are goddamned fine people.

"I talk with colored people a lot," he said, "with the elevator operators, the shoeshiners and in the parking lots, and do you know what they say? They don't buy all this (militant) crap."

Reactions to the story were swift and numerous. In phone calls and letters to the editor, readers either questioned what a man with Felicetta's views and demeanor was doing on the Human Relations Commission or wondered what a "family" newspaper like the *Tribune* was doing by printing such language. The majority seemed to be more concerned with the latter point than with Felicetta's place on the Human Rights Commission.

From its standpoint the paper could point out that a Human Relations Commission member's use of such language may be newsworthy and that the story as a whole gave a good picture of Felicetta and his praiseworthy community activities. An editorial in the *Tribune* also noted that Felicetta's views were probably similar to those of many other Minneapolis residents and that service on the Commission could be a good experience for him.

Critics of the paper could argue that the *Tribune's* editorial policy was opposed to Mayor Stenvig and that his appointee suffered as a result. The paper might "clean up" or omit vulgarities mouthed by officials it favored but sought to discredit the Stenvig appointee, it was argued.

In a *Tribune* staff memo following the controversy, the issue was reviewed; many of the memo's points are worth re-stating here as a summary:

> We can't lay down a hard-and-fast policy. We can't answer all the questions and solve all the problems. But we can and must depend upon the good judgment and maturity of the staff to understand the problems involved and to make carefully considered decisions. . . .
>
> . . . Consider the source of the quote and the circumstances. If use of an obscene or vulgar word is necessary to accurately convey the meaning and impact of a significant comment on a significant subject, we print it.
>
> Ask yourself. Is this a responsible person speaking on a significant subject? Will we miss the flavor and impact of his quote if we launder it? If the answer to both questions is yes, use the exact quote. . . .
>
> [but]
>
> We want to cover the news fairly and squarely and without squeamishness. But we must remember that we are a mass medium with a conservative audience and our responsibility goes very far in informing that audience.
>
> We don't inform readers when we make them angry. We turn them off, no matter how important the story may be. In their current mood, readers are ready to jump on us for anything. We have too much to do that is important to afford to alienate readers.
>
> Profanity and obscenity are facts of life these days. We should not pretend that we have just discovered them. Any good story can be written around such language without losing its point—and the story will be read. But there is always that rare exception. . . .
>
> [and a concluding thought]
>
> A good test is examination of motives. If we have a good and responsible reason for what we do, we need not be ashamed of it nor fear criticism . . . let's discuss these situations as they come up.[10]

Suppose in another case a news source grants permission for an interview, discloses private information about himself, and then—before the story is published—revokes all consent and asks that the information he gave voluntarily not be used. What should the reporter do?

One thing the reporter might do is go to the company lawyer for advice. This is what happened when such a situation occurred at *Sports Illustrated*. The lawyer decided the story could be published; the news source sued for $6 million for invasion of privacy.

In California, U.S. District Judge Gordon Thompson, Jr., who first thought the plaintiff merited a hearing, reversed himself in late December 1976 because the incidents reported about the news source were considered to be newsworthy and not morbid prying into the private life of Mike Virgil.[11] The story, published February 22, 1971, was "The Closest Thing to Being Born" and concerned body surfing near Newport Beach, California. Virgil, a body surfer, had willingly told author Thomas Curry Kirkpatrick things that led Kirkpatrick to write that Virgil "is considered to be somewhat abnormal." Virgil would put out a cigarette in his mouth, burn a dollar bill on the back of his hand, and dive headlong down a flight of stairs to impress some girls. The standard of newsworthiness that Judge Thompson considered notes:

> In determining what is a matter of legitimate public interest, account must be taken of the customs and conventions of the community; and in the last analysis what is proper becomes a matter of community mores. The line is to be drawn when the publicity ceases to be the giving of information to which the public is entitled and becomes a morbid and sensational prying into private lives for its own sake, with which a reasonable member of the public, with decent standards, would say that he had no concern.[12]

The judge said the newsworthiness test "avoids unduly limiting the breathing space needed by the press for the exercise of effective editorial judgment."

In other reporting situations the question may not be the language of the news source or the fact that the news source, having given information, now requests that it not be published.

Increasingly there are instances when the news source agrees to be quoted but does not want to be identified. This leads us to consider when news sources should be protected for the benefit of the news audience.

To Aid the News Audience

Earlier we discussed the trend toward taking the role of the reporter more seriously. Just how seriously is indicated by the willingness of many reporters to go to jail rather than to identify news sources or yield information acquired on a confidential basis and, in the legal process, for news companies to spend thousands of dollars in the courtroom battles. Much of the history of American journalism of this generation has been written in courtrooms as judges, prosecuting attorneys, and lawyers considered to what extent the First Amendment and state "shield laws" provided news reporters the privilege of not divulging information sought by grand juries, police, and other law enforcement and judicial agencies.

The issue is not peculiar to this century. In his autobiography Benjamin Franklin told of being summoned to a court to testify about a story in the *New England Courant,* edited by his brother James. Ben would not talk, and the court did not press the issue.[13] What is peculiar to this century is the number of subpoenas issued to reporters, the number of shield laws now passed by state legislatures, and the impacts of court decisions on news reporter–news source relations.

The point at issue is in some ways simple and yet profound: The system of government in the United States requires an informed electorate capable of self-government. That is one of the ends to be served by the First Amendment. In the process of providing information to the citizenry, reporters at times must guarantee to the news source that his or her identity will not be revealed or that some information learned in the news-gathering process will never be divulged. Professor David Gordon put it this way:

> What is involved is the public's right (rather than privilege), exercised via the news media, to be kept informed of what is going on in society. Both protection of confidential sources and safeguarding of confidential information relate directly to the credi-

bility of a newsman in the eyes of his sources. This affects the ability of that reporter—and of others faced with similar demands by their sources—to keep the public informed. On controversial issues, reporting is likely to be forced into imbalance if one side does not trust the media enough to provide information on its activities or beliefs. Without such knowledge about all aspects of society, voters become less able to govern themselves rationally. This is the basic reason for any newsman's privilege.[14]

Generally reporters have used three defenses to protect the anonymity of news sources and the confidentiality of information: (1) They argue that the First Amendment in guaranteeing freedom of the press also protects the newsgathering process and that freedom of the press is violated when legal authorities seek to coerce reporters to identify sources or divulge information. (2) Shield laws now enacted in about half the states provide protection to reporters and their sources. (3) The willingness of reporters to go to jail rather than to disclose news sources—civil disobedience if you will—also is an option.

News sources sometimes need the assurance that the reporter is willing to go to jail or that the law will protect confidentiality of sources and information. It is easy to illustrate that some news sources may suffer when they disclose information.

Here is what you might call a minor case, told by simply quoting from a story published in the Grand Forks, North Dakota, *Herald* of Wednesday, February 26, 1975.

A part-time city employe who provided information to the *Herald* for a story on security at the airport was fired the day after the story appeared.

Hal Adams, who worked as an accountant in the office of Airport Manager Norman Midboe, was fired Saturday, after a *Herald* story quoted from a letter he had written to Midboe in November alerting airport employes to federal security regulations.

Adams said Midboe never distributed the letter.

About a month later, Charles Donald Stewart, 26, allegedly attempted to hijack an airline after driving through an open freight gate, which was supposed to have been locked.

> The city on Tuesday tentatively agreed to pay a $1,000 federal fine for leaving the gate open.
>
> Adams said city officials have told him that he was fired because he "overstepped his bounds" by writing the letter and was suspected of talking to the *Herald.* . . .
>
> Adams was dismissed without notice.
>
> Midboe told the *Herald* he was "not really satisfied" with Adam's work and added that the dismissal "didn't have anything directly to do" with the article.
>
> "Why should I tell you to begin with?" he asked. "I shouldn't have to explain why I dismiss a part-time employe."
>
> Adams said he spoke to the *Herald* because he "felt a moral obligation to myself and the city."

A far more celebrated case was the 1969 firing of A. Ernest Fitzgerald by the U.S. Air Force about a year after Fitzgerald had testified about cost overruns in the development of the costly C-5A Galaxy jet transport. Fitzgerald, deputy for management systems in the Air Force, had told a Senate subcommittee chaired by Senator William Proxmire that cost overruns on the giant transport would be $1 billion to $2 billion.

Fitzgerald's case and his battle to regain his job are discussed in some detail in reporter Clark Mollenhoff's book, *Game Plan for Disaster.* Air Force denials that Fitzgerald was fired because of his testimony before a congressional subcommittee do not seem to hold up.

> The Air Force, displeased by Fitzgerald's frankness, initially denied the accuracy of his figures. Then they conceded that the contract arrangement had not lived up to its much publicized origins and reluctantly admitted that new agreements were underway and would guarantee Lockheed substantial profits [on the C-5A].[15]

The Nixon administration, which took office after Fitzgerald had testified, did not support him. In the Watergate hearings in the summer of 1973, a January 1970 memo surfaced regarding the Fitzgerald case. The memo was to H. R. Haldeman, President Nixon's right-hand man, from Alexander Butterfield, an Air Force colonel, who was a White House aide.

> Fitzgerald is no doubt a top-notch cost expert, but he *must* be given very low marks in loyalty; and after all, loyalty is the name of the game.
> Only a basic no-goodnik would take his official business grievances so far from normal channels.
> We should let him bleed for a while at least. Any rush to pick him up and put him back on the federal payroll would be tantamount to an admission of earlier wrongdoing on our part.[16]

In one of the ironies of Watergate, Butterfield was to find himself in a situation which to some appeared similar to Fitzgerald's. It was Butterfield who, in answer to a question, told the staff of the Watergate Committee in July 1973 that President Nixon had a secret taping system in the White House for "historical purposes." Butterfield had worked with the Secret Service in getting the system installed.

Earlier in 1973 he had been named administrator of the Federal Aviation Administration by Nixon. When he was asked to resign that post by President Gerald Ford in 1975, Butterfield believed it was delayed retribution for his disclosure of the existence of the tapes.

Butterfield's 1970 memo about Fitzgerald—particularly the choice of words "let him bleed"—came back to haunt him when the Senate considered whether to restore him to the rank of colonel. (He had to resign from the military to become head the FAA.) The rank was not restored. Some senators argued that separation of military and civilian authority should not allow officers to resign commissions to work as civilians and then be restored to rank when they quit the civilian jobs. With return to the military closed to him, Butterfield also found it difficult to be reemployed as a civilian. Doors that logically should be open to a former assistant to a President of the United States may have been closed because of his disclosure about Nixon's tapes.

Fitzgerald, Adams, and Butterfield did not seek anonymity. But their cases—particularly Fitzgerald's and Adam's—suggest why some other persons do.

Public employees often are the sources of information about misdeeds, errors, and corruption of higher-ranking public officials. Because of the employees' vulnerability—the threats to job security and promotion they may face for reporting such misdeeds—it is understandable that such employees request anonymity when talking to reporters. If reporters are unable to assure such anonymity, the news sources are less likely to talk and the corruption will continue, unreported and unabated. Senator Lowell Weicker of Connecticut said as much when he spoke on the Senate floor, urging (unsuccessfully) passage of a federal shield law:

> I might add that one of the provisions of this bill provides that news sources cannot be revealed in cases "involving abuse of power by public officials." Why? The answer is simple. With minor exception research shows that every major scandal in public office over the past 20 years was uncovered by the press. Sometimes, it seems, we must look outside our government for help in uncovering government abuses. If we didn't protect this news we might never hear about these abuses again. This is so important that it must never be discouraged.[17]

It also is argued that without a reporter's privilege to keep confidential some news sources and information, the views of many dissidents and the so-called disenfranchised would not reach the public. The media provide a forum for those whose political views and activities virtually preclude them from holding public office or having access to other public forums such as appointed committees and civic organizations. The constitutional logic here is that in our system of government it is important for all segments of society to know what others are thinking and that a sizable portion of our society is likely to have an incomplete view if not provided some access to the views of minority and dissident groups. To deny access of such groups to the news media may only foment violence.

This point was raised in 1800 by Tunis Wortman, a New York lawyer, and discussed by Leonard Levy in *Freedom of Speech and Press in Early American History: Legacy of Suppression:*

> Men whose only guilt consists of credulity, zeal, prejudice, mistaken opinion, or "imbecility of understanding" are victimized by prosecutions with the

> result that the free formation of public opinion is destroyed and a pernicious silence creeps over society. . . . Indeed, by damming up discontent and removing the possibility of its verbal expression, prosecutions make a resort to violence more likely.[18]

The shield law issue, however, like many involving First Amendment protection of the press, is not as clear-cut as much of the preceding discussion might lead you to believe. There is not even near unanimity among news reporters on the related questions as to whether they should have shield laws or whether shield laws are necessary. Those who argue against shield laws point out that journalists traditionally have opposed special privileges for any class of society and that shield laws for reporters are inconsistent with this tradition. They also note that irresponsible and unscrupulous reporters might abuse shield laws by making unsubstantiated charges and accusations and then claiming a right to protect a source who, for all anyone knows, is fictional.

Nor do all journalists applaud when a state passes a shield law.[19] They reason that if a state legislates a shield law, the state can unlegislate just as well, leaving the journalist worse off than ever. Another argument by opponents of shield laws is that anything less than an absolute shield law protects reporters only in situations stated by the law, leaving them unprotected in all other situations. They suggest that the First Amendment, a journalist's willingness to go to jail, and the development of trust between reporters and their sources are sufficient—if not the best—guarantees for anonymity and confidentiality of information.

The case of the Fresno Four speaks to the fickleness of a state shield law. The California shield law provides that news reporters "cannot be found in contempt by a court, the legislature, or any administrative body for refusing to disclose the source of *any information*" procured for publication and published in a newspaper" (emphasis added).

That seems explicit enough. Yet George Gruner (managing editor of the *Fresno Bee*), James Bort (city editor at the time of the offense), and reporters Bill Patterson and Joe Rosato spent two weeks in jail in 1976 for refusing to tell a judge the source of their information about grand jury testimony regarding alleged bribery involving a city official. The information was furnished to the paper, the four acknowledged, by someone not bound by an order issued by Judge Denver Peckinpah to not discuss the case with the news media. Still, after a lengthy court battle, the four spent time in jail because Judge Peckinpah said the legislature could not tell him how to run his courtroom and the state supreme court declined to hear the appeal.

Since the status of shield law legislation and court interpretations of the First Amendment will change through the years, what relatively stable guidelines exist for the reporter in terms of serving the news audience and respecting news sources requests for anonymity?

1. Pledges to keep material confidential or to keep the source of the information anonymous should not be made lightly. Some news organizations require reporters to inform editors or managing editors of such pledges, to assure that the news medium is willing to support the reporter and others involved in the story through whatever legal actions might follow.

2. The duty of all citizens to testify in court is deeply rooted in our system of government, as is the right of the accused to confront those making charges against him. No court or grand jury is likely to waive these duties and rights merely to satisfy ill-founded or whimsical requests by reporters to keep sources of information confidential.

3. To provide access of all segments of society to the news media and to adequately inform the news audience about what is happening in their society, reporters must from time to time guarantee news sources that their identity will be kept secret and that some information will be kept confidential. When such guarantees are made, the reporter and the employer accept the consequences.

4. Not all requests for anonymity have to be studied under a legal microscope. Daily reading of a newspaper will suggest to anyone that reporters routinely grant anonymity to sources in reporting a wide range of items, from baseball locker room talk to conversations in a Senate cloakroom. In many of these cases, the tests are whether the information is useful to the news audience, whether the request for anonymity is a reasonable one, and whether the information is also available from some other source who would not request anonymity.

PROMOTING NEWS SOURCES

Twenty-five years ago sociologists Paul Lazarsfeld and Robert Merton introduced the concept of "status conferral" in a discussion of media effects. They observed:

> The mass media confer status on . . . persons. . . . Enhanced status accrues to those who merely receive attention in the media, quite apart from any editorial support. The mass media bestow prestige and enhance the authority of individuals and groups by legitimizing their status. Recognition by the press . . . testifies that one has arrived.[20]

As James Lemert and others have observed, the concept of status conferral is an articulate rendering of the old show business or political line: "I don't care what they say about me, as long as they spell my name right."[21]

Lazarsfeld and Merton suggested that the course of public debate on social issues and the emergence of spokesmen and leaders on those issues may depend in large part on whom the media use as news sources. Equally important, as recognized by the press in more recent years, is that the nature of the debate also is shaped by whom the media do *not* use as sources.

If we understand promotion of a news source to mean enhancement of the reputation, power, and prestige of the source, it might be instructive to consider a few ways in which the newsgathering process confers such benefits on news sources and issues. Inherent in the notion of status conferral is a cyclical process that would go like this: Because a news source is quoted in the paper, speaking out on a certain issue, that news source gains increased recognition and status; because of that increased recognition and status, the news source is sought by reporters for comment when the issue arises again.

Because a news reporter is sometimes only as good as his or her sources, the reporter may benefit when the source he or she relies on becomes more widely recognized and quoted by others. It may also happen that a young reporter turning in a story without a quote from a person who has been quoted on the issue before may be asked to phone the established news source for comment too. You can almost hear the city editor:

"We can't have a story on ———— without a comment from
————. She's been in all our other stories."

A resource used often by reporters is the newsroom library,
which often includes clippings from previous issues of the newspaper, filed by subject matter and by name of the news subject.
A reporter given an assignment to cover a city event or issue
need only check the clippings on the issue or event to learn the
background and who the recognized news sources are.

Often the news media are accused of biased news coverage,
plainly—in the critic's eye—favoring one high school football
team or one political candidate over another. Newsrooms often
are intrigued and amused by what readers or viewers divine as
complicated conspiratorial plots to favor a certain issue or individual. Occasionally reporters receive complaints of biased
reporting from both sides on an issue, each complaining the
other was favored.

Our discussion on informing, protecting, and promoting
news sources should at least suggest that the subtle complexities
of the reporting process and the competence of the reporter may
do more to shape what is reported than any heavy-handed conspiracy.

Recommended Readings
    For additional information on shield laws, the following are use-
ful:
    Francois, William E. *Mass Media Law and Regulation*. Columbus,
Ohio: Grid, Inc., 1975.
    Gora, Joel M. *The Rights of Reporters: The Basic ACLU Guide
to a Reporter's Rights*. New York: Avon Books, 1974.
    "Is the First Amendment in Jeopardy?" *Columbia Journalism Re-
view*, Sept/Oct 1972, pp. 18–37, with a 12-page supplement on the
opinion of the U.S. Supreme Court on the shield law cases of Earl
Caldwell, *New York Times;* Paul Branzburg, *Louisville Courier-Journal;* and Paul Pappas, WTEV–TV, New Bedford, Mass.
    "Newsmen's Privilege Legislation," an analysis by the American
Enterprise Institute for Public Policy Research, Washington, D.C.
Other recommended readings:
    Bernstein, Carl, and Woodward, Bob. *All the President's Men*.
New York: Simon and Schuster, 1975.
    Krieghbaum, Hillier, *Pressures on the Press*. New York: Thomas
Y. Crowell, 1972.
    Levy, Leonard W. *Freedom of Speech and Press in Early Ameri-
can History: Legacy of Suppression*. New York: Harper & Row, 1963.

MacDougall, Curtis D. *The Press and Its Problems.* Dubuque, Iowa: William C. Brown Company, 1964.

Mollenhoff, Clark. *Game Plan for Disaster.* New York: W. W. Norton, 1976.

Wicker, Tom. *A Time to Die.* New York: Quadrangle, 1975.

5 Traditional and nontraditional news sources

Traditional news sources are defined here in operational terms, the ways news media have gathered most of their information this century. Most of the news has come from (1) beats or official news sources, (2) public relations or promotional agencies and personnel, and (3) attendance of reporters at events defined as newsworthy.

Some relatively newer, varied, or more popular approaches to newsgathering in recent years include (1) "precision journalism," (2) the enactment and use of freedom of information laws, (3) use of anonymous or veiled sources, and (4) use of minority group members and dissidents as news sources. For sake of contrast we call these nontraditional sources, granting that some have been around for a long time but recognizing an increase in their use in recent years.

Discussions in this book about interviewing; pitfalls awaiting the reporter; and informing, protecting, and promoting news sources are relevant to both traditional and nontraditional sources. Changing the sources of information does not automatically lessen the likelihood of biased, incomplete, or inaccurate reporting. Changing the sources of information may, however, affect the context in which reporting problems occur. It should be instructive to review the older and newer sources of news and consider how use of them might affect what is reported.

BACKGROUND STORY

© 1967, Herblock, in the *Washington Post*

BEATS

Listing typical news beats is akin to saying the words "mom" and "apple pie." A list of beats is a recitation of social and political institutions generally revered and respected for their roles in our society: the courthouse, city hall, school board, church, police and fire departments, business, real estate, sports, fraternal organizations, the legislature, and others depending on local industries and governmental agencies.

Even a cursory reading of the list should suggest why it is convenient, and perhaps necessary, to structure at least part of the news coverage in such fashion. Beats are predictable and continuing sources of news in terms of the effects they have on our lives and the services they are supposed to provide. The day-to-day occurrences on beats are well suited to satisfying such news criteria as proximity, prominence, timeliness, consequence, conflict, and human interst.

News from a beat generally is continuing and interrelated: action taken in May is related to action in December; Tuesday's comments are related to Thursday's arguments. Consequently it is useful to have the same reporter covering a beat over a period of time. Thus the beat system helps assure the news audience of informed coverage that is placed in perspective with the news source's past actions and future options.

At its best the beat system provides the news audience with informed reporting of issues and events likely to affect the lives of the readers and viewers—from the increase of taxes to public services financed by the collection of those taxes. The beat system also lends itself to newsroom organization and a division of labor according to the competence, interests, and abilities of the reporters.

Defects of the beat system emanate from the source of its strength: continuing coverage by the same reporter. Familiarity with the the news beat and news sources, sympathy with the sources' problems, and a sense of responsibility for the success of the sources' programs may become the overriding concern of the reporter—to the point of being confused with responsibility to the news organization or the news audience. Such concern is an understandable result of prolonged and thoughtful communication between a news source and reporter, but the concern may give the reporter a distorted perspective.

Harrison Salisbury and Jimmy Breslin talked about this on Salisbury's public television program *Behind the Lines:*

> SALISBURY: I think that newspaper reporters in general tend to float up above the real people of this country. Do you think that's true?

> BRESLIN: Absolutely. I think that's why we only had two fellows that did the Watergate reporting . . . Woodward and Bernstein. Everyone else in Washington goes to dinner with news sources.[1]

Relationships between reporters and news sources who see one another almost daily will differ from relationships between reporters and news sources who meet or talk on the telephone only once. The reporter in the former situation, by almost all that is known about human behavior, will seek at least cordial relationships with the continuing news source. The long-term result of such behavior is likely to be less critical and unbalanced news coverage.

At times when a news medium is working on a controversial story that will put a regular news source in a bad light, a reporter other than the one who routinely covers the source is assigned to write the story. The reasoning is that the news medium does not want to jeopardize the long-term relationship between the beat reporter and his or her sources.

When public agencies differ, the differences may be reflected in the newsroom. A city editor seeking to understand what is happening between the chief of police and the city manager is likely to get different accounts from the reporter who regularly covers the police and the reporter who covers city hall and the city manager.

When a beat reporter goes on vacation and another reporter replaces him or her even for a week or two, curious and sometimes humorous things result. School board members accustomed to a cozy and informal relationship with a beat reporter—a relationship built over a period of years—may continue that behavior when covered by the relief reporter. They may be astonished and embarrassed when they read the coverage of their meeting and learn that the interim reporter has written about what the regular reporter ignored. The reader or viewer gets a markedly different view of an agency because of changes or variations in the beat system.

Few reporters have the chutzpah attributed to Mel Mencher, now a journalism professor at the Columbia University Graduate School of Journalism. When Mencher was a reporter for the *Fresno Bee*, he helped write a series of articles that led to the election defeat of Mayor C. Cal Evans. When it was clear that the mayor would not be reelected (the story goes), Mencher sauntered into the mayor's office, sat down in front of his honor's desk, propped his feet on the desk, and said matter-of-factly: "Looks like you're dead, C. Cal." Mencher it should be noted, was not the regular city hall reporter.

Several things can be done to take advantage of the strengths of the beat system and limit its defects: city editors and managing editors may regularly rotate reporters on beats to assure some turnover and a well-rounded staff; reporters and desk personnel might also rotate; copy editors and others should edit news stories mindful of possible reporter bias; reporters on the beats should seek professional relationships with news sources—relationships based on the accuracy and completeness of reporting and not on the favorability of the news; the news medium can complement coverage of traditional news sources with so-called nontraditional sources to achieve a degree of balance in its coverage.

PUBLIC RELATIONS, PROMOTIONAL PERSONNEL

It is ironic that news sources supplying so much of the material and information for the news media should be in as much disfavor as are public relations firms and promotional agencies.

Most reporters who have been aided by public relations and publicity personnel carry embarrassing scars or bad memories because of inaccurate or incomplete information, telephone calls that were not returned or (purposely?) were returned too late, or the inability to talk directly with the company president. The result has been an increasing gap between reporters and public relations people. More reporters now buy their own meals and cups of coffee; and many news operations now pay their reporters' admission to ballparks, theaters, and other places where reporters must go to cover newsworthy events.

On the other side of town, a feeling of growing hostility has been apparent in many board rooms. There are presidents and executives who won't talk to the press because of what they perceive as sloppy, limited, inaccurate, or biased reporting. "All they ever want to write about are our holdups and embezzlements," lamented one bank president, upset because he couldn't get any coverage of a widely acknowledged accomplishment in urban affairs programming by his organization.

The mutual distrust and resentment have existed for years and are not likely to change overnight. Shoddy, unthinking, and incompetent public relations people remain on the loose; so do journalists whose skills and judgments do their profession and the news audience a disservice.

On the other hand, there are hundreds of public relations/ publicity personnel whose careful work has won deserved praise. And some public relations and advertising practitioners have left jobs because they refused to be associated with organizations that were about to market untested or possibly dangerous products or because their principles did not permit them to make unsubstantiated claims about certain products. There also are universities employing what appear to be highly moral people to teach public relations skills—with few of them being accused of teaching students the art of the cover-up.

Why then is there such controversy over public relations? Perhaps one reason is that the reporter and editor, president and press representative are "too busy" to give much thought to what he or she might do to make the news source–news reporter relationship better and more productive for the news audience.

The news side really may not know, care, or understand very much about the public relations business. The phrase public relations, or PR, has come to mean one thing: publicity, the free ride. Probably few reporters think of public relations in terms of the Public Relations Society of America, which sponsors numerous workshops and an accreditation program to upgrade the standards of the profession; few think of public relations personnel as ombudsmen, arguing for more disclosure or social action programs by their employers. Reporters are, however, likely to remember the corporate president who tried to hide poor earnings in the last paragraph of a four-page news release, the college president who told his secretary to say he was out of town, the agency that sent in 200 pages of meaningless news every month or so, or the public relations director who denied a merger just hours before it was formally announced.

Mistakes that business, government, and association executives make in their media relations probably come from pressure—pressure to cover up a problem, to make earnings seem better, to outdo the competition. Obviously this does not excuse the actions. It does suggest the nature of "human thinking" behind a news release. And in many instances such decisions may be contrary to the advice of the public relations counsel.

The fact is that numerous successful businessmen and

businesswomen do not know how to communicate. They compound the problem by hiring amateurs—many of them ex-reporters—who are not competent to draw long-term public relations goals and objectives and, as a result, head for the typewriter and demonstrate their prowess by the volume of their press releases. Much of their output winds up in newsroom wastebaskets, sometimes in unopened envelopes.

The attitudes a reporter forms about people who send him or her reams of useless material probably are reinforced by the classroom and newsroom image of public relations personnel as space grabbers who have sold their souls for money. Also journalism periodicals often carry articles about the efforts of people to withhold significant information from the press, about businessmen who withdraw advertisements because of unfavorable news stories, or about letters-to-the-editor campaigns organized by public relations personnel.

It might be tempting to conclude that the journalist has nothing to gain from public relations personnel. In evaluating this position, probably the one certainty is that public relations people do have a mission: to tell the story of and promote the organizations that issue their paychecks. That mission is not necessarily inconsistent with being helpful to reporters. In fact, public relations personnel who are helpful to reporters—and that includes being informative, open, and honest—are often those of most value to their employers. Reporters serve the news audience better by knowing and understanding an organization's public relations program and personnel. It would be folly to write off an organization or its potential news value simply because of stereotypes about public relations in general.

So while it may not be easy to be objective about the relative news value in the news releases flooding news desks each each day, it may be useful to think of those releases as just one element in relations between publicity personnel and reporters. Reporters can do some things to make the relationships benefit the news audience:

1. Realize that the public relations person has a mission (to tell the story of the employer) but realize also that the mission does not necessitate a big swindle or a free ride. Accurate information about a company's products, number of employees, major marketing areas, and public service programs often is useful to readers; and competent public relations personnel can provide

it. Such information may be useful in stories about the economy, consumer consciousness, and societal trends.

2. Approach the newsgathering situation with a degree of good faith and become acquainted with public relations personnel with whom he or she might deal on a regular basis. There is a difference between being open-minded and being naive, just as there is a difference between being skeptical and questioning instead of being cynical and disbelieving. Readers are served better by open-minded but skeptical and questioning reporters. As in dealing with other news sources, it is helpful for reporters to talk with public relations sources even when not working on a specific story or seeking specific information. Such informal contacts may give a reporter a competitive edge when working on a breaking news story and, in the long run, will make the reporter a better judge of a source's credibility and lead to a better understanding of the context in which the source operates.

3. Apprise news editors of what appears newsworthy, regardless of its source or potential free advertising message. It is sometimes surprising where news stories begin. James Risser's Pulitzer Prize-winning expose of corruption in the grain trade began when he read a routine press release from the U.S. Department of Agriculture about indictments of five grain inpectors in Houston, Texas. Reporters reading press releases see angles that those who prepared the releases might have missed. Further, a release that puts someone in a positive light should not be automatically discarded as puffery. An innovation in farm machinery, for example, may have far-reaching implications for the nation's economy and social structure.

4. Be cautious and thorough in dealing with press releases, as in working with all news stories. That seems too obvious to merit comment here. Yet it is almost routine to see in *Columbia Journalism Review* and other periodicals collections of news stories that appeared in several newspapers but were the same word for word. All were verbatim reprints of public relations releases. Rewriting news releases is important and useful for a number of reasons: omissions of information or inaccuracies are more likely to be noted than if the release is merely edited or run as is; rewriting makes the story appear different from the version used by others; rewriting may necessitate contacting sources to acquire additional information or to verify the information in the release; rewriting often reduces the space needed

to publish the release's news. In sum, rewriting serves the interest of the reader better than running the news release as it arrives in the mail.

A summary of the above four points is that it should be the responsibility of the reporter—not the public relations person—to determine what is reported to the news audience. The public relations person can be a valued aid in that process but should not control it.

ATTENDANCE AT NEWSWORTHY EVENTS

In addition to obtaining news material from beats and public relations aides, reporters gather news by attending events considered newsworthy: public meetings, football games, fires, fairs, flower shows, accidents, riots, conventions, and so forth. Such coverage is essential. It is what much of reporting will always be about. The reporter gathers news firsthand by observing the event rather than hearing about it from a news source. Beyond that the strengths of on-the-spot coverage are in its timeliness, human interest, and proximity.

Shortcomings are involved in such coverage, however. For one thing, coverage by attendance at events is similar to the beat system, because many of the events are public meetings or other scheduled happenings that represent points of view similar to those expressed by "officialdom." In deciding what events to cover, the newsroom relies on many of the criteria used in establishing the beat system.

Many news sources have learned to manipulate the news media, contriving what have been termed "pseudo events"—events designed merely to attract media coverage. News conferences rank high in the list of pseudo events.

A third shortcoming of such coverage is that it finds the media primarily *reacting*, chasing to get to where the action is to report it. The conflict orientation in news—defining what is news in terms of conflict and disturbance—leads to this form of coverage.

After the civil disturbances of the 1960s many news editors and directors recognized that readers and viewers would be served better by the reporting of issues, trends, and problems in society than by coverage of the turmoil that results when problems remain unsolved for a long time. For example, a detailed look by the news media at the causes, results, and treatment of drunken driving might be of more value to the news audience than the daily recitation of drunken driving arrests, accidents, and deaths.

While many of the foregoing comments about traditional news sources tend to be negative, it should be clear that reliance on such coverage is unavoidable and necessary. So we do come out in favor of "mom" and "apple pie." Such news coverage, however, remains only a part (granted, a large part) of the total picture. To make the picture more complete and more accurate, newer approaches have been introduced.

PRECISION JOURNALISM

"Precision journalism" was a term coined to represent the introduction of social and behavioral science research techniques into news reporting. The use of such research methods, it is argued, is needed and timely.

The case for improving reporting methods is well made in *Precision Journalism, A Reporter's Introduction to Social Science Methods* by Phillip Meyer and in *Handbook of Reporting Methods* by Maxwell McCombs, Donald Shaw, and David Grey.

In his opening chapter, "The Need for New Tools," Meyer writes:

> It used to be said that journalism is history in a hurry. . . . [T]o cope with the acceleration of social change in today's world, journalism must become social science in a hurry. . . . The ground rules are no different from those on which we've always operated: find the facts, tell what they mean and do it without wasting time. If there are new tools to enable us to perform this task with greater power, accuracy and insight, then we should make the most of them.[2]

McCombs et al. write of translating reporting goals and tasks into the framework of behavioral science studies:

> Our central premise is that this translation will enhance the quality of news reporting in two ways. First, behavioral science methodology makes possible a whole realm of description that is simply not feasible using the traditional interview or paper-and-pencil techniques of interviewing. . . . Second, news reporting is also enhanced by behavior science meth-

ods that lead the reporter beyond description to explanation.[3]

The new tools and new methods these authors write of include survey research, random samples, sensitive interviewing techniques, and field experiments.

There are two reasons for reporters to acquaint themselves with these newer methods: (1) use of such methods can improve the accuracy and reliability of sampling public opinion; (2) even if reporters are not using these methods, others are.

As to the first point, with the increased use of computers in newsrooms and the availability of relatively inexpensive computer time, use of survey research approaches the convenience of sending two or three reporters out on man-in-the-street interviews. Survey research also promises far more accuracy. Further, a field experiment can be something as simple as testing the efficiency of zip codes through systematic mailing of letters with and without the five-digit codes.[4]

Second, even if news agencies do not adopt these methods, reporters need to be better acquainted with them for the sake of the news audience. Almost any political candidate or interest group nowadays can cook up a poll or study to "document" widespread public support. Reporters need to know enough about research techniques to evaluate the newsworthiness of such findings and to tell readers and viewers why some data are questionable.

Using the tools of the social and behavioral sciences is not new to the newsroom. The importance of employing reporters well grounded in sociology, political science, economics, psychology, and history has long been recognized. Reporters knowledgeable in these areas provide the news audience with a better news report. Using the newer tools of these disciplines seems a logical step for reporters to take.

To belabor the obvious, the so-called new tools are not panaceas. Use of survey research and field experiments brings new problems and does not automatically eliminate problems of reporter-source relations previously discussed. Reporters enamored of survey research, for example, may immerse readers and viewers with irrelevant information. We already have political campaign coverage that tells us who would win if so-and-so were running against such-and-such in an election held today. But neither of them is running and the election is not "today" but two years hence. High-powered tools incorrectly used may only bring high-powered reporting mistakes more difficult for the news audience to discern. A considerable burden remains on the reporter for wise use of reporting methods when he or she moves, as McCombs et al. say, "beyond description to explanation."

PUBLIC RECORDS, FREEDOM OF INFORMATION LAWS

Public records include those musty accounts and government documents supposedly filed away in the basements and attics of bureaucracy. More often public records are those available for inspection by reporters with the time and interest to study them to complement news coverage of public agencies and public officials. News reporters often may be too source-oriented to recognize the value of, say, checking census data to see if they are consistent with what local officials say about housing conditions, educational levels, or incomes in a community.

Attention to such public records in recent years has grown because of the work of consumer advocate Ralph Nader, because of mistrust of public officials (or, if not mistrust, the commendable desire of reporters to verify the public pronouncement of officials), and because of the access to records provided by the federal Freedom of Information Act and state "open records" and "open meetings" laws.

In 1971 Julius Duscha, director of the Washington Journalism Center, discussed the work of Ralph Nader's workers. The weakness of reporters, Duscha wrote, was that:

> . . . in Washington and elsewhere, the press is almost totally oriented to reacting to events, or, in too many cases, to psuedo events carefully contrived for press coverage. . . . [T]he hundreds of reporters who make up the Washington press corps still spend an inordinate amount of time serving up rewrites of White House and agency handouts, once-over-lightly accounts of legislative maneuverings and meaningless "scoops" on the size of the Federal budget to be announced officially tomorrow. . . .
>
> . . . Nader and his forces are doing no more than what good reporters are supposed to do. His operations are what good newspapering ought to be all about. . . . First must come the extensive study of the background of an issue, largely through research in books, articles, Congressional reports and official documents. Then follows the interviewing

of key sources to discover as much as possible about the current situation. Finally, there are the conclusions to be drawn and the courses of action to be charted.

Why is the press generally unwilling to do the kind of in-depth investigative work that is the guts of the approach to public issues by Nader and his aides? The major reason is the way editors and reporters are oriented toward the reporting of events.[5]

Clark Mollenhoff, former Washington bureau chief for the *Des Moines Register* and *Tribune* and winner of the 1958 Pulitzer Prize for national reporting for an expose of labor union racketeering, argues forcefully that reporters should dig into public records. He notes that time invested in reading federal budget data is likely to be far more productive than time spent establishing inside, anonymous sources who will offer tips. What makes this form of reporting so productive, says Mollenhoff, is that few reporters make good use of public records.

Use of public records is on the increase, however, thanks in part to new dimensions added by the enactment of the Freedom of Information Act in 1968 and its 1974 amendments, effective February 19, 1975. In surveying the results of the FOI Act to mid-1976, George Lardner, Jr., a reporter for the *Washington Post*, noted:

> It is burdensome. It is costlier than expected. And it is working far more effectively than anyone imagined when Congress enacted it despite Mr. Ford's veto [of the 1974 amendments]. . . .
>
> For the first time, federal officials are supposed to respond within fixed deadlines to requests from "any person" for government documents. For the first time, officials face disciplinary action for any arbitrary or capricious withholdings.[6]

Robert Woodward and Carl Bernstein of the *Washington Post* used the FOI Act to gain access to government records showing that the once-powerful Ohio Congressman Wayne Hays used his office to benefit relatives and friends at taxpayers' expense. Beset by his scandal with paramour Elizabeth Ray and other problems, Hays, a 15-term representative, decided not to seek reelection in 1976 and then resigned from the House before the election.

James Risser of the *Des Moines Register* points out that the FOI Act also protects some civil servants. If a lower-rung civil servant voluntarily provides a reporter with information that puts a government agency in a bad light, that public employee may be punished by his superiors. But if the information is provided to comply with federal or state law, the employee is blameless.

While the more dramatic changes in freedom of information laws in recent years may have been in the 1974 revisions of the federal statute, there remain strong concerns regarding open records and open meetings laws at the state and local levels. After all, most news reporters work at the local and state levels, and decisions by these government agencies usually have more immediate effects on citizens. A school district's decision to close an elementary school has more immediate and personal impact than a congressional decision to increase tax exemptions by $150, for example.

Every state except Rhode Island has some form of open meetings law. The most recently enacted was New York's, which took effect January 1, 1977. Forty-five states have open records laws. Delaware, Vermont, and West Virginia have no such law; Rhode Island and Mississippi have laws providing for some open records at the local or county levels.[7]

The arguments for open records and open meetings laws are straightforward yet profound. Our system of government requires an informed citizenry. If that citizenry is to be informed and if the government is to be accountable, there must be access to the decisions made by government agencies and the opportunity to participate in the decision-making process. In short, public business should be conducted publicly.

Typically, proponents of open meetings and open records laws want nothing so exotic as the secret to the H-bomb. Rather there is a desire to know why one paving contract was accepted over another, why a new teacher will be added in physical education instead of in music, why a certain person was selected to complete the unexpired term of a city councilman who resigned. These may seem mundane matters, yet such decisions affect the lives of millions of citizens each day. The public has a need to know and to meet that need there must be effective open meetings and open records laws.

Laws vary from state to state. Tennessee's open meetings law says that all gatherings of two or more members of a governing body of any public agency, except by chance, are to be open. Not much room for doubt there. On the other hand, an Iowa law said meetings should be open unless there was a two-thirds vote to close the meetings for discussion of personnel or real estate matters or for a "reason so compelling" as to override the general policy in favor of public sessions. "Compelling" reasons to close meetings are easy to manufacture and difficult to battle in court.

Existence of freedom of information laws is one thing; enforcement is another. A strong open meetings law is worth little if the news media of the state do not regularly cover meetings of state and local agencies or do not seek enforcement of the law when it is violated. A healthy freedom of information climate requires at least good legislation, aggressive use of that legislation by news reporters, and public understanding and support of the philosophy behind open meetings and open records laws.

To adequately cover the news, reporters need access to public records and public meetings. That goes without saying. How much access do reporters need, however, to secret or anonymous sources?

ANONYMOUS SOURCES

The necessity and value of using anonymous sources from time to time in news reporting was discussed in the previous chapter, as part of our review on protecting news sources. Let us now consider more of the problems involved in the use of such sources.

Charles Seib, ombudsman for the *Washington Post,* discussed in an August 1975 column the increased use of anonymous sources. He referred to research by Professor Hugh M. Culbertson of Ohio University on the use of anonymous sources:

> [T]he concealment of news sources . . . is a game stacked against the public. The press and the insiders usually know who is leaking what. . . . Only the customers are kept in the dark.
>
> A few decades ago, the "informed source" and the unnamed "high official" were rare birds. But today these shy but knowledgeable fellows are everywhere. . . .
>
> Culbertson's sampling . . . showed that the bigger and more prestigious the newspaper, the more it used unnamed sources. The New York *Times* and

the Washington *Post* used them in 54 percent of their
stories during the period studied. Four other large
newspapers used them in 36 per cent of their stories.
But six small dailies used them in only 30 per cent.

The Culbertson study indicates that perhaps
one-third of the news stories read by the American
public rely wholly or in part on sources known to the
reporter and perhaps his editors, but not to the
reader.[8]

Anonymous sources may be public officials or news sources
found on traditional news beats, who—for one reason or another, perhaps their own convenience—find it more useful to
try to speak off the record. Seib discussed this in January 1976:

Anonymous sources are part of the news business. Seldom does a day go by without at least one
major news story in which they figure. There is no
reason to think that situation will change.

But there is a question that can and should be
asked: Have reporters and their editors become too
comfortable with anonymous sources? And that leads
to some other questions:

Does not the public have a right to expect a
story . . . to contain some information on the motivation of those who leaked it?

Why can't such a story indicate at least a gen-
eralized source, even though confidentiality of the individual is preserved? Did it come from Capitol
Hill? Or the State Department? Or the White House?
Or several places?

Do reporters try hard enough to get sources to
allow their names to be published? If a congressman
decides that it is in the public interest to disclose a
piece of information, should he be willing to have
his name appear with it? And if not, should he give,
for publication, an explanation of why not?

This whole business of sourcing is closely related
to the subject [of] . . . manipulation. As long as the
press is willing to accept material from anonymous
sources and to print it without disclosure of the circumstances under which it was obtained, manipulation will flourish. "Scoops" that serve special purposes, laudable or otherwise, will abound.[9]

Seib's concerns about anonymous sources are well taken. Of
all the news sources considered in this chapter, those requesting
anonymity should be regarded most warily by reporters. For one

thing, as Seib points out, the reader deserves information to help in evaluating the credibility of the message. For another, a news source may become less responsible if he or she knows that no name will be linked with the information reported.

There are different types of anonymous sources of course. Most reporters should be able to distinguish between a source requesting anonymity for protection against retaliation by those he or she exposes and a source requesting anonymity to avoid being connected with self-serving pronouncements or with dubious criticism of a political rival. Often, however, it may not be so easy to discern the motivation for the request for anonymity.

For the reporter and the news audience there are some guidelines to consider in using anonymous sources, in addition to those suggested by Seib.

1. The reporter should corroborate information from an anonymous source. Even other anonymous, independent sources might be used. This was the practice followed by Woodward and Bernstein in much of their Watergate reporting. They sought two or three separate and independent confirmations of information provided by anonymous sources.

2. Articles relying on anonymous sources generally should carry the by-lines of the reporters. Responsibility for the content of news stories, including the comments of anonymous sources, must rest someplace. In addition, the reporter's by-line may give the discerning reader some yardstick for gauging the credibility of the story. (Culbertson's studies, by the way, have suggested that the news audience does not necessarily find anonymous sources less credible).

3. Anonymity should not be the first resort of a reporter when dealing with a news source. If the news source seems hesitant about answering a question, the reporter has options other than blurting out, "Well, I'll keep your name out of it, if you want." If the source is a public official, the accountability of such officials to the public should be stressed. If the source is not a public official, the reporter might stress reluctance to use comments from an anonymous source. Out of modesty, for self-preservation, or for less worthy motives, many news sources might jump at the chance to be quoted anonymously; the reporter should not so tempt the news source at the first sign of reluctance.

There are good reasons for the use of anonymous sources, but the list of such reasons does not include making the reporter's job easier.

MINORITIES AND DISSIDENTS AS NEWS SOURCES

Traditional sources of news and even some nontraditional sources are weighted toward the "establishment" or, what is less pejorative, the majority point of view or the *status quo.*

Thirty years ago, in its study of press freedom, the Commission on Freedom of the Press said one of the requirements of the media was to project "a representative picture of the constituent groups in the society." The commission's concern was that some groups were stereotyped in the media:

> If the Chinese appear in a succession of pictures as sinister drug addicts and militarists, an image of China is built which needs to be balanced by another. If the Negro appears in the stories published in magazines of national circulation only as a servant, if the children figure constantly in radio dramas as impertinent and ungovernable brats—the image of the Negro and the American child is distorted.[10]

In recent years the concern has been not only with stereotypes in reporting but also with assuring access to the media so that minority groups might find in the media the opportunity to participate in making the decisions that affect their lives, thereby improving their lot. Concern with minority groups became almost an emergency item in the 1960s when, after riots in urban centers, editors surveyed their newsrooms and papers and discovered: (1) there were not many minority group reporters and (2) the media had not done a very good job of covering the issues and problems that helped lead to the unrest. As a result several programs were instituted to recruit and train minority group members for journalism careers.[11]

Minority group members need not be defined solely in terms of color, race, age, or sex. In broader terms the news media have been called on to provide access to the media for those affected by government decisions in addition to the existing access for the decision makers.

To this end, law professor Jerome Barron has argued for a new interpretation of the First Amendment. Barron's argument, summarized briefly, is that the freedom of speech and press provided by the First Amendment is not enough to assure that citizens will be heard. The commercialization of the media and the decline in newspaper competition concentrates more influence in fewer hands. Barron says the legislature and the judiciary should guarantee not only freedom of speech and press but also access to the media—the vehicles for such expressions.

> New forms of dialogue are necessary. What I propose is to implant these forms on an existing structure. I would not substitute government control of the media for their present private ownership. What I suggest is that the media be rendered more hospitable as a routine and legal matter to diversity of viewpoints. . . . Interchange of ideas will not arise naturally and without new procedures. Economic and technological factors have become such constraints on the life of ideas that the *laissez-faire* Millsian approach to freedom of expression . . . is now a hopeless anachronism. But the democratic faith in reason . . . is still the basic assumption of our institutions. Unless we are ready to discard this faith, we should give considerable attention to the idea of access and to attempts to realize that idea through new legislation and more intensive and sympathetic use of existing law.[12]

While Barron argues for the legislature and judiciary to guarantee access, Tom Wicker of the *New York Times* has argued along different lines—for placing responsibilities on reporters and editors—but reached a similar conclusion:

> [W]e have to . . . overcome or at least reduce and balance our reliance on official sources of news, which I regard as the gravest professional and intellectual weakness of American journalism. . . . A chairman of the Democratic National Committee speaking about the Democratic party will—as an example—be given greater credence than some obscure political scientist. . . . A President is automatically presumed to know more about foreign relations than a senator or an academic. . . . [These] assumptions are not necessarily warranted.[13]

The most glaring example of why these assumptions are not necessarily warranted is the Vietnam war, Wicker said. But the problem is one of local, not global, concern:

A lot of what's happening in the country today, a lot of what is most vital in people's lives, isn't institutionalized so there's no official spokesman for it. If you stick to covering the official sources, inevitably you miss a lot of important things that are going on elsewhere. So, for instance, the press largely missed one of the great migrations of human history, the migration of black people out of the South and into the cities, until Watts blew up in 1965. And until Ralph Nader made something sensational out of it, we missed the rise in consumer consciousness; now, ironically, we've made something of an official source out of Ralph Nader. It's the way we like to work.[14]

"The way we like to work" introduces to the news coverage of minority news sources problems similar to those involved in covering the traditional news sources. For example, in the brief history of the news media's coverage of the civil rights movement, a continuing theme has been the media's search for *"the* black leader." Just who was *the* spokesman for America's blacks? Martin Luther King, Jr., Elridge Cleaver, Whitney Young, Ralph Abernathy, Stokely Carmichael, H. Rap Brown, Huey Newton, James Farmer, Roy Wilkins, Julian Bond, Jesse Jackson?

It was almost a news media version of the television show *To Tell the Truth,* with the media asking the real black leader to "please stand up." The point was slowly learned that there might not be any black leader who could speak for all blacks, any more than there was one white spokesman, or even one city councilman who could speak for the entire city council. Before some reporters learned this, however, the authenticity of a black leader's ability to speak for other blacks was determined in part by the amount of violence he urged. A black leader saying a city should be burned down was defined as more authentic than one who would be content if one block were burned.

That may seem a bit facetious, but the news media had difficulties at times in making the adjustment from traditional to nontraditional sources of news. For the news reporters and the news audience there should be some satisfaction if diversity of viewpoints is represented in the media. Representatives of various points of view are difficult enough to find without worrying about seeking "the" spokesman for an interest group. Also it should be remembered that no news medium and few news stories rely on solitary news sources. A combination of sources—news beats, public records, precision journalism—can be used to inform readers and viewers rather than relying on the dubious use of one or two persons representing socially acceptable or, on the other hand, extreme points of view.

As with other problems in reporting, the issue of who is a "legitimate" or "worthwhile" news source does not go away. It merely reappears from time to time in different settings. A current question is news media coverage of terrorists and terrorist activities. Certainly a major news story of the 1970s and perhaps beyond will be terrorist activities as more airplanes are hijacked, more hostages are slaughtered, and more threats are made to gain support for one dissident cause or another. The question of coverage of terrorist organizations is a complex one, particularly when considered with the concept of status conferral discussed earlier. In considering press coverage of terrorism, the following comments may be useful:

> Public unease in a democratic state must be allayed by proper publicity on the need for countermeasures [to terrorism], so that the psychological means and tactics employed by the terrorists, and their aim of sapping the government's civilian support, can be thoroughly understood. This is especially important when and if it becomes necessary to call in military aid, which may be essential in view of the advanced weaponry available to contemporary terrorists.
>
> The terrorist side has often used the media to great advantage. Nothing serves the cause of terrorists better than a glamorized "clandestine" interview with hooded men, filmed expressly for television. It is the duty of those seeking to protect the public against the gunman and the bombthrower to enlist the cooperation of media personnel with a view to a fair presentation of the need for countermeasures in the common interest. Terrorists should not be allowed to get away with the pretense that they are spokesmen for legitimate pressure groups.[15]

These comments are provocative. Serious questions are raised when the media are considered to be an arm of the government in combatting terrorism. On the other hand, few can object to the concluding thought that terrorists should not be allowed to deceive the public into thinking they have widespread and sympathetic support if they do not.

TV Guide, which often offers perceptive commentary on issues involving the news media, offered these insights on terrorism and television:

> [T]errorist groups, however, are still cavorting on the world stage, and TV news organizations are regularly faced with tough decisions about how to handle them. No serious critic says that censorship is the answer. . . . If TV withholds legitimate news of violent acts, rumor will take over . . . and become a worse problem. . . . "The terrorists will have won," says a State Department official, "if we throttle our free press in the attempt to minimize terrorism. It would be like grounding all our commercial airliners to discourage potential hijackers."[16]

Some critics, however, do question the role the media play:

> "Ninety per cent of these events are the homespun efforts of bumbling dum-dums tryng to make names for themselves," says psychiatrist Dr. David Hubbard. "They wouldn't even *think* of bombing and hijacking, unless you guaranteed them a rostrum. If the media cut their coverage down to the importance of other minor news, these men wouldn't act."[17]

If the comments of Dr. Hubbard seem familiar, they are. In different contexts his comments have been heard before as critics of the media warned of press coverage encouraging imitation of criminals, of television violence urging children to go and do likewise, of press coverage making it impossible for a person to get a fair trial, of press coverage of noisy minority groups only encouraging them to further disruptive tactics, of all the problems and troubles that might go away if only the news media would not pay so much attention to them.

The National News Council, however, flatly rejected the suggestion that the news media should not cover terrorist activities. At its March 1977 meeting in Des Moines, council members said they rejected "as unthinkable any notion that such activities should not be reported because they are perceived as 'contagious.' " They continued:

> The dangers of suppression should be self-evident: doubts over what the media have withheld and the motives for such a blackout; questions about other types of news which might also have been withheld ostensibly in the public interest; and the greater possible risks involved in wild and reckless rumors and exaggerated, provocative word-of-mouth reports.

That there has been irresponsible coverage by the media no one will deny. But coverage of a city council meeting can be as irresponsible as coverage of a riot or a kidnapping. The apparent immediate effects are less easy to discern perhaps, but in a system of government based on an informed electorate, continuing irresponsibility of media coverage on any important subject will be pernicious.

The answer is not to have less news coverage or none at all. The answer is to have better news coverage. The ingredients of that better coverage must include new and varied approaches to news sources and reporters more sensitive to the nuances of the reporting process.

Recommended Readings

Bagdikian, Ben H. *The Information Machines: Their Impact on Men and the Media.* New York: Harper and Row, 1971.

Baker, Robert K., and Ball, Sandra J. *Violence and the Media,* Staff Report of the National Commission on the Causes and Prevention of Violence. Superintendent of Documents, U.S. Government Printing Office, 1969.

Balk, Alfred, and Boylan, James, eds. *Our Troubled Press.* Boston: Little, Brown and Company, 1971.

Becker, Howard S. *Outsiders: Studies in the Sociology of Deviance.* New York: Free Press, 1963.

A Free and Responsible Press. New York: Twentieth Century Fund, 1973.

Ghiglione, Loren, ed. *Evaluating the Press: The New England Daily Newspaper Survey.* Southbridge, Mass.: *The Evening News,* 1973.

MacDougall, A. Kent, ed. *The Press: A Critical Look from the Inside.* Princeton, N.J.: Dow Jones Books, 1972.

Merrill, John C., *Existential Journalism.* New York: Hastings House, 1977.

Merrill, John C., and Barney, Ralph D. *Ethics and the Press: Readings in Mass Media Morality.* New York: Hastings House, 1975.

Park, Robert E. *On Social Control and Collective Behavior.* Edited by Ralph H. Turner. Chicago: University of Chicago Press, 1967.

———. *Society: Collective Behavior, News and Opinion.* Glencoe, Ill.: Free Press, 1955.

NOTES

CHAPTER ONE NOTES

1. A June 17, 1976, lecture sponsored by the Newspaper in the Classroom project of the *Des Moines Register* and *Tribune* and the Drake University Bicentennial Committee.

CHAPTER TWO NOTES

1. Walter Lippmann, "Stereotypes," *Public Opinion* (Free Press, New York, 1965), pp. 54–55.
2. Raymond Bauer, "The Initiative of the Audience," *Journal of Advertising Research,* June 1963, pp. 2–7.
3. "The Mind of an Assassin," *First Tuesday,* broadcast on NBC television network June 3, 1969.
4. The role of James Gordon Bennett in developing the modern concept of news is discussed in most journalism history textbooks and also in "Park Revisited: A New Look at the 'Natural History of the Newspaper,'" a paper read to the history division of the Association for Education in Journalism, Aug. 1967, by Professor Walter Gieber of San Francisco State University.
5. One good McCarthy reference is Richard H. Revere, *Senator Joe McCarthy* (Harcourt, Brace and Company, New York, 1959).
6. The seventh edition of *Interpretative Reporting* was published by Macmillan in 1977. A Golden Anniversary edition is planned for the early 1980s.
7. Commission on Freedom of the Press, *A Free and Responsible Press* (University of Chicago Press, Chicago, 1947).
8. Leon V. Sigal, *Reporters and Officials: The Organization and Politics of Newsmaking* (D. C Heath and Company, Lexington, Mass., 1973), p. 7, quoted from a panel discussion at the Institute of Politics, Kennedy School of Government, Harvard University, May 19, 1970.
9. Telephone interview with James McCartney when he was city editor of the *Chicago Daily News,* May 6, 1968.
10. Jules Witcover, *White Knight: The Rise of Spiro Agnew* (Random House, New York, 1972), p. 364.

CHAPTER THREE NOTES

1. "The Case of the Plastic Peril," *CBS Reports,* broadcast on CBS television network Oct. 19, 1974, with CBS News Correspondent Morton Dean.
2. Bob White, "Maryland: Getting the Governor," *Columbia Journalism Review,* July/August 1975, pp. 12–14.

3. Eugene J. Webb and Jerry R. Salancik, *The Interview or The Only Wheel in Town*, Journalism Monograph No. 2, Association for Education in Journalism, University of Minnesota, Nov. 1966; Eugene J. Webb et al., *Unobtrusive Measures: Nonreactive Research in the Social Sciences* (Rand McNally & Company, Chicago, 1966).

4. Edward T. Hall, *The Silent Language* (Fawcett World Library, New York, 1967); Julius Fast, *Body Language* (M. Evans, distributed through Lippincott, New York, 1970).

5. "Controversial Comments," *Wall Street Week* #435, Mar. 28, 1975, Maryland Center for Public Broadcasting, Baltimore.

6. Richard W. Lee, ed. *Politics and the Press* (Acropolis Books, Washington, D.C., 1970), p. 59.

7. *Meet the Press*, Aug. 10, 1976, Vol. 19, No. 32, Merkle Press Inc., Washington, D.C.

8. Webb and Salancik, pp 28–34.

CHAPTER FOUR NOTES

1. Ben Hecht, *Gaily, Gaily: The Memoirs of a Cub Reporter in Chicago* (Doubleday, New York, 1963), p. 226.

2. Roy Fisher, "The Challenging Role of the Newsman," *Nieman Reports*, Sept. 1972, p. 14.

3. William L. Rivers, *The Adversaries* (Beacon Books, Boston, 1970), p. 69.

4. Hecht, p. 2.

5. When reporters confront such situations as informing a news source about a death—particularly by phone—it may be advisable to determine whether the news source is alone, perhaps even to phone a neighbor to assist the person in a time of grief. It does no good to hang up or to cut the conversation short and not share at least some information with the news source. A reporter might ask some questions, depending on the circumstances, or make arrangements to phone back or phone someone else.

6. Dennis Cassano, "AP suspends man for giving FBI information," *Minneapolis Tribune*, Apr. 16, 1974, p. 1B.

7. Harley Sorensen, "AP photographer in Wounded Knee case is fired," *Minneapolis Tribune*, Apr. 20, 1974, p. 6A.

8. Michael Gartner, "Editing a family newspaper in a campaign rated 'R,'" *Des Moines Sunday Register*, Oct. 10, 1976, p. 1-D.

9. Jack Miller, "Public official speaks his mind," *Minneapolis Tribune*, Sept. 15, 1969, p. 1A.

10. *Minneapolis Tribune* Staff Memo No. 54, Sept. 19, 1969 (which included excerpts from staff memos of June 13, 1969, Aug. 1, 1968, and Sept. 15, 1969).

11. "Judge Reverses Himself; Dismisses Privacy," *Editor & Publisher*, Jan. 8, 1977, p. 10.

12. *Michael S. Virgil v. Time, Inc.*, United States District Court for the Southern District of California, 527 F 2d 1122.

13. Benjamin Franklin, *The Autobiography of Benjamin Franklin* (Random House, New York, 1950), p. 24.

14. David Gordon, "The Confidences Newsmen Must Keep," *Columbia Journalism Review*, Nov/Dec 1971, p. 15.

15. Clark R. Mollenhoff, *Game Plan for Disaster* (W. W. Norton and Company, New York, 1976), p. 66.

16. Ibid., p. 72.

17. *Congressional Record*—Senate, Jan. 11, 1973, S442.

18. Leonard W. Levy, *Freedom of Speech and Press in Early American History: Legacy of Suppression* (Harper and Row, New York, 1963), pp. 287–88.

19. State legislatures that have passed shield laws include those in Alabama, Alaska, Arizona, Arkansas, California, Delaware, Illinois, Indiana, Kentucky, Louisiana, Maryland, Michigan, Minnesota, Montana, Nebraska, Nevada, New Jersey, New Mexico, New York, North Dakota, Ohio, Oregon, Pennsylvania, Rhode Island and Tennessee.

20. Paul Lazarsfeld and Robert Merton, "Mass Communication, Popular Taste and Organized Social Action," *Readings in Social Psychology,* rev. ed. (Holt, New York, 1952), p. 76.

21. James Lemert, "Status Conferral and Topic Scope," *Journal of Communication,* Mar. 1969, p. 4.

CHAPTER FIVE NOTES

1. *Behind the Lines*—Guest: Jimmy Breslin, Host: Harrison E. Salisbury, broadcast nationally on the Public Broadcasting Service Mar. 2, 1976.

2. Philip Meyer, *Precision Journalism* (Indiana University Press, Bloomington, 1973), pp. 14–15.

3. Maxwell McCombs, Donald Lewis Shaw, and David Grey, *Handbook of Reporting Methods* (Houghton Mifflin Company, Boston, 1976), p. ix.

4. Ibid. pp. 265–66.

5. Julius Duscha, "Nader's Raiders Put the Washington Press Corps to Shame," *The Progressive,* Apr. 1971, pp. 24–26.

6. George Lardner, Jr., "Freedom of Information Act: Burdensome, costly, much used," *Washington Post,* July 25, 1976, p. A3.

7. Information on state and local Freedom of Information laws is from the 1976 *Report of the Advancement of Freedom of Information Committee* of the Society of Professional Journalists, Sigma Delta Chi, and from "A Summary of Freedom of Information and Privacy Laws of the 50 States," *Access Reports,* Richard Henry, ed., Washington, D.C. My thanks to Professor William Francois of Drake University's School of Journalism for his help here and in other sections dealing with communication law.

8. Charles Seib, "Concealing news sources: Game stacked against the public?" *Washington Post* News Service, *Des Moines Register,* Aug. 25, 1975. The Culbertson study is reported in the ANPA News Research Bulletins No. 3, May 14, 1975, and No. 1, May 19, 1976.

9. Charles Seib, "Is press manipulated by its 'Confidential' sources?" *Washington Post* News Service, *Des Moines Register,* Jan. 21, 1976.

10. Commission on Freedom of the Press, *A Free and Responsible Press* (University of Chicago Press, Chicago, 1963), p. 26.

11. Information regarding journalism careers for minority group members is available from American Newspaper Publishers Association, PO Box 17407, Dulles International Airport, Washington, D.C., 20041; and The Newspaper Fund, Inc., PO Box 300, Princeton, N.J. 08540.

12. Address on "Access—The Only Choice for the Media," given at the annual lecture on Law and the Free Society at the University of Texas School of Law, Dec. 10, 1969, and reprinted in 48 *Texas Law Review,* 766, 769–71 (1970). This particular quote is from *Mass Media Law and Regulation* by William E. Francois (Grid, Inc., Columbus, Ohio, 1975), pp. 355–56.

13. Tom Wicker, "The Reporter and His Story: How Far Should He Go?" *Nieman Reports,* Sept. 1972, pp. 15–16.

14. Ibid., p. 17.

15. "Terrorism Can Be Stopped," *Skeptic,* Jan/Feb 1976, pp. 46–47, excerpts of a report by the Institute for the Study of Conflict, London.

16. Neil Hickey, "Terrorism and Television, The Medium in the Middle," *TV Guide,* Aug. 7, 1976.

17. Ibid.

NAME INDEX